BRADFORD WEST GWILLIMBURY P. L.

938
.9
Mat

May 01, 2018

D0856973

Sparta

Sparta

Rise of a Warrior Nation

Philip Matyszak

DISCARDED
BRADFORD WG
PUBLIC LIBRARY

Pen & Sword
MILITARY

Bradford WG Public Library
425 Holland St. W.
Bradford, ON L3Z 0J2

To the memory of Diana Tansley

First published in Great Britain in 2017 by
PEN & SWORD MILITARY
an imprint of
Pen & Sword Books Ltd
47 Church Street
Barnsley
South Yorkshire
S70 2AS

Copyright © Philip Matyszak, 2017

ISBN 978 1 47387 464 0

The right of Philip Matyszak to be identified as Author of
this Work has been asserted by them in accordance with the
Copyright, Designs and Patents Act 1988.

A CIP catalogue record for this book is available from the
British Library

All rights reserved. No part of this book may be reproduced
or transmitted in any form or by any means, electronic or
mechanical including photocopying, recording or by any
information storage and retrieval system, without permission
from the Publisher in writing.

Printed and bound in Malta by Gutenberg Press Ltd

Pen & Sword Books Ltd incorporates the Imprints of Pen
& Sword Aviation, Pen & Sword Maritime, Pen & Sword
Military, Wharncliffe Local History, Pen and Sword Select, Pen
and Sword Military Classics, Leo Cooper, Remember When,
Seaforth Publishing and Frontline Publishing.

For a complete list of Pen & Sword titles please contact
PEN & SWORD BOOKS LIMITED
47 Church Street, Barnsley, South Yorkshire, S70 2AS, England
E-mail: enquiries@pen-and-sword.co.uk
Website: www.pen-and-sword.co.uk

Contents

Glossary

Agathoergi – A picked group of 300 'enforcers'

Agelai – a 'herd' of Spartan children in training

Agoge – the Spartan education system

Archagetai – the Spartan kings

Aspis – hoplite shield

Doru – Hoplite spear

enomotia – file of warriors in the battle line

hebontes – young men in the final stage of training

homoioi – 'The Equals' Spartan men in good standing

hippagretai/hippeis – royal bodyguard

kleroi – plots of land held by Spartiates

Kopis – sword type

linothorax – armour type

obai / phylai – division of the Spartan people

paiderastia – 'love of boys'

paides – stage of the *agoge*

perioiki – free non-Spartan Lacedaemonians

phratry – aristocratic faction

Phoebaeum – a ritual fight

Spartiates – fully paid-up Spartan warriors

syssitia – Spartan communal mess

Xiphos – sword type

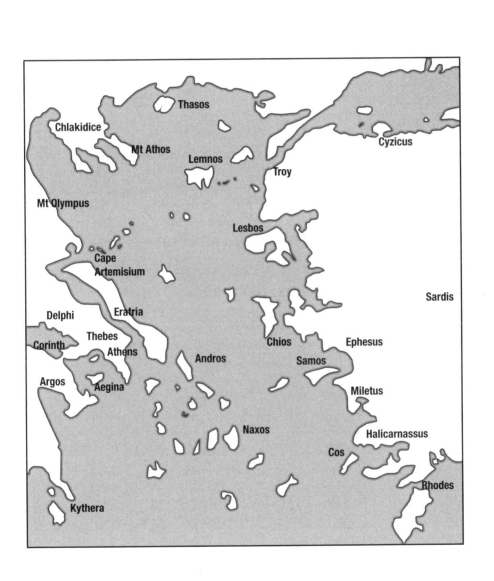

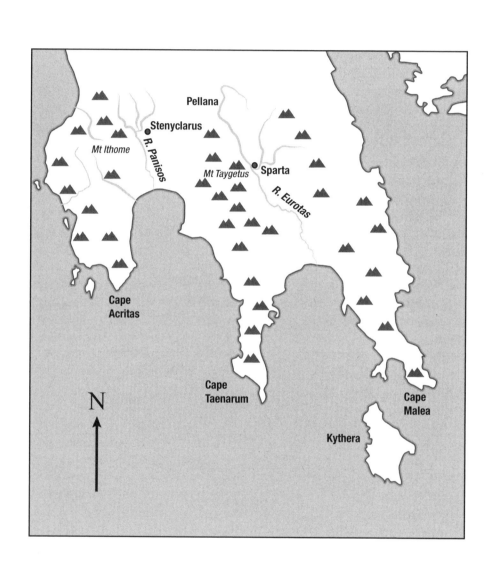

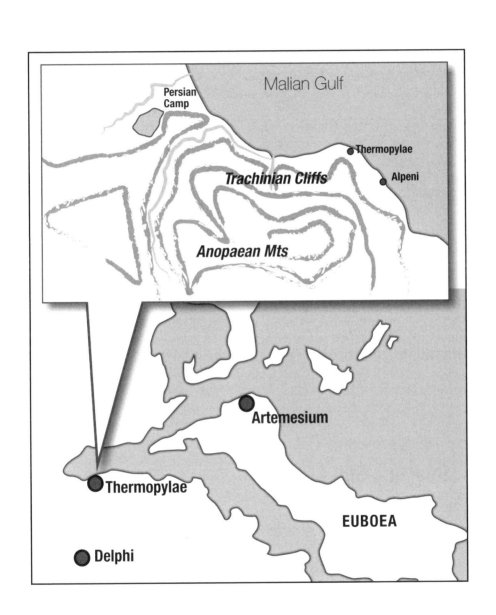

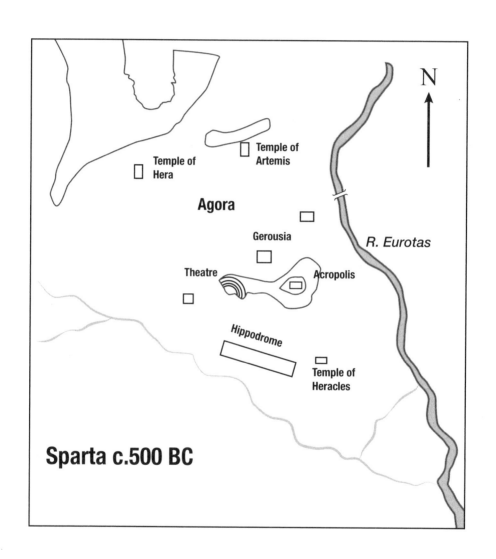

Sparta c.500 BC

Chapter One

This is Sparta

Putting it in perspective...

Imagine a Persian ambassador in the year 492 BC. His master is Darius, the King of Kings. Darius' domains stretch eastward from the shores of the Mediterranean to the Indus River, taking in the lands of modern Turkey, Syria, Jordan, Israel, Egypt, Iran and Iraq and encompassing goodly chunks of other lands as well. The population of this empire numbers in the tens of millions. The ambassador has come to demand the submission of the city-state called Sparta, in the territory of Laconia in Greece.

Rounding the peninsula of Cape Malea, the most south-easterly point of the Peloponnese, the ambassador's ship arrives at the little harbour where the River Eurotas meets the sea. The Lower Eurotas runs through a valley just 17 miles in length and 4 miles wide. Even from his ship at one end of the valley, the ambassador can clearly see the mountains at the valley's other end. Disembarking, he asks one of the locals, 'Are you a Spartan?'

'No,' comes the reply. 'I am a *periokos*, one who lives in the vicinity of Sparta. Sparta is two-thirds of the way up the valley, on the western side.'

'Seriously?' the ambassador must have asked himself. 'Here am I, from a mighty empire, come to demand homage from a city-state so tiny that it can completely fit into the grounds of just one of the king's hunting estates without seriously interfering with the livestock. How can this fly-speck of a city possibly defy me?'

Even now, given how large the legend of Sparta looms in the modern consciousness, it is still astounding how small Sparta actually was – in modern terms it has about the area and population of the small town of Ely near Cambridge in the United Kingdom. Even contemporary Greeks noticed that Sparta was remarkably unremarkable.

'I suppose if Lacedaemon [Sparta] were ever to be abandoned, and nothing but the temples and the foundations of the buildings remained, later eras would refuse to believe the city was as powerful as its reputation. ... The city is neither compact form nor boasting magnificent temples and public buildings. Rather it is a collection of villages in the old Greek style, and it all would seem rather inadequate.'

Thucydides *History of the Peloponnesian War* 1, 10.

Sparta was situated in the south-east of the Peloponnese, and this southern peninsula of Greece is itself just 8,278 square miles – one tenth the size of Turkey across the Aegean Sea. Furthermore, most of the Peloponnese is barren mountain rock, with spaces for human settlement being few and far between.

The geography of the Peloponnese had a profound effect on the history and psychology of the Spartans, so in examining the development of their extraordinary state, we should pay close attention to Sparta's physical surroundings.

The Peloponnesian peninsula can be best imagined as the right paw of a massive dragon placed in the Mediterranean Sea. The dew-claw of this dragon's paw is the Argolid peninsula in the north-east. Above that and more central lie the lands of Achaea and Corinth. To the west at the top of the paw is Elis, the land that for over a millennium hosted the eponymous games at Olympia.

In the centre lies the upland mass of Arcadia, an area with an average elevation of over 2000 feet above sea level, elaborately folded into a series of mountain ranges, and small, fierce streams in deep ravines and hidden valleys. Indeed so much geography has Arcadia that little space remains for history which has largely passed the region by, making Arcadia a modern metaphor for a timeless bucolic paradise.

For the Spartan historian, the Peloponnese gets really interesting as we approach the southern end, where the dragon's claw extends three roughly equidistant talons southward towards Africa. The eastern talon is Malea, the central is Tainaron, and the western talon is stubby Akritas. Like knuckles behind each talon, there lies a mountain range behind, and extending into, each peninsula.

The 'knuckle' which interests us most is behind the central peninsula of Tainaron. This is the Taygetos Range, the highest peak of which is Mount Taygetus. This mountain has a hugely significant role on our story, and is, incidentally the oldest named peak in Europe (thanks to a mention by Homer in the *Odyssey*). The Taygetos Range itself is significant because the valley to the east, watered by the river Eurotas, comprises the fertile part of Laconia wherein Sparta lies. To the west, on the other side of the Taygetos Range, flows the parallel Pamisos River. The land around the River Pamisos is Messenia, a region both flat (by Peloponnesian standards) and highly fertile (ditto), divided in two by a single intruding mountain range.

This brisk geographical survey shows that while all of the Peloponnese is pretty small, the area of Laconia – mountains and all – takes up less than a quarter of the whole; being some 1,500 square miles in total. Or to put it another way, after mastering Laconia, Sparta dominated an empire about 49 miles long and 35 miles wide. To expand further, the Spartans had to either get through the Taygetos Range to the west, the inhospitable mass of Arcadia to the north, or take their chances with the open sea. Note though, that the ancient Mediterranean was mostly closed to navigation in the winter months, and though Sparta itself seldom saw snow, enough fell on the Taygetos Range to make crossing the passes very difficult. For much of the year, Laconia was basically cut off.

To these physical barriers were added psychological ones. The same obstacles that made it hard for Sparta to break out of Laconia made it equally difficult for anyone else to get in. With isolation, Sparta developed an insular, parochial outlook, a sense of being different and special. Much as Sparta later became enthusiastic about projecting Spartan power as far afield as possible, the city's rulers were well aware that this had to be done while projecting abroad as few actual Spartans as possible. Outside their own unique society Spartans had a distressing inability to control themselves, let alone any putative subject peoples. Therefore, no matter how great a power the city was to become, mentally it remained a small mountain-bound state buried in the side of the Taygetos massif.

Origins part I. Archaeology

Who were the Spartans? Where did they come from? There are

two answers to this question. Though both answers agree on certain points, they are very different; though both are 'true' according to the perspective of the person making the inquiry.

Human settlement in the Peloponnese goes well back into prehistory. Archaeologists have discovered sites almost 50,000 years old. The first humans who occupied these sites came through the narrow Isthmus of Corinth, and formed tight, isolated communities in the sheltered valleys between mountain ranges. However, even the archaeological picture of these first hunter-gatherer settlements is patchy until the agricultural revolution of some 8,000 years ago. Life in Laconia would have been far from easy for these early farmers. But at least the climate was mild, conditions were good for agriculture (assuming one had limited ambitions concerning the size and diversity of harvests) and the mountains limited both the number of predators and raids from warlike fellow-humans. A summer drought with rainfall in spring and autumn made the location suitable for two grain harvests a year, a crop cycle which continued into the classical era.

Many settlements were not permanent – poor understanding of land use meant that low-quality soils were easily worked out and eroded, and a fluctuating climate brought its own problems. (In 2015 archaeologists found a complete prehistoric city underwater off the coast of the Argolid, submerged by changing sea levels.) Nevertheless, some sites were long settled, and appear to have endured for millennia. The valley of the Eurotas was one of the most fertile in Greece, and settlement here was relatively dense. Pottery shards and commonality of artefacts show that the various settlements of Neolithic Laconia were aware of each other's existence and that trade took place both between villages in the Eurotas valley and between Laconia and other regions of the Peloponnese.

Most settlements along the Eurotas valley were on the western side, where detritus washed from the Taygetus mountain massif created a fertilized stretch of land already enriched by the deposits of a long-extinct inland sea. The eastern side of the river had a thinner strip of land created by silt from the river itself. Most of the valley is less than 5 miles wide, and the mountains looming on either side of the river explain the name given to the area by the poet Homer – 'Hollow Lacedaemon'. The alluvial coastal plain, today one of the richest farming areas in the valley, did not exist in prehistoric times and indeed, some indications suggest that the coastal area was so dry and barren that the main occupation of the inhabitants was sheep-herding.

If Sparta existed at this point, the inhabitants left little for later archaeologists to discover. The earliest reliable indications of permanent settlement come from the Bronze Age which began around 3000 BC. A stream called the Magoula flows from the Taygetos Range to meet with the Eurotas River, and on the east bank opposite is a high rocky spur called Therapne, and a now-abandoned settlement which archaeologists call the Menelaion. This was on the opposite side of the river from where classical Sparta later arose. There was a prehistoric settlement called Amyklai on the Spartan side, but this appears to have been a satellite settlement of the Menelaion, the hilltop of which was at its prime fully covered with houses and surrounded by a defensive wall. Unlike the Menelaion, Amyklai remained inhabited into the classical era and became one of the several satellite villages which made up 'metropolitan' Sparta.

The hill of the Menelaion was an important centre in early Bronze Age Laconia, and it became increasingly important as time went on. It was not the dominant city of the region however – that honour went to Pellana. Pellana (today a tiny village) sits at the top of Laconia, whereas Sparta lies almost in the middle. Dominating access to the Eurotas valley from the rest of Greece, Pellana may have been the regional 'capital' – although that term can only be loosely applied to the much devolved society which appears to have existed at this time. As the Mycenaean kingdoms of Greece grew and became more centralized, the capital of the kingdom of Lacedaemon might have been either Pellana or the Menelaion – the matter is still disputed. Archaeology shows that one of the earliest Mycenaean palaces in mainland Greece was built at the Menelaion – and demolished shortly afterwards, which suggests that the matter of primacy might also have been hotly discussed in prehistoric times.

Archaeology can tell us little about the politics and customs of the people who lived in the area. We know that warfare was an issue, both because Mycenaean Greeks appear to have pursued the pastime with enthusiasm and because the archaeology of contemporary sites in Laconia show that the builders had a deep interest in defence. We also know that the Menelaion was a religious centre from very early in the Bronze Age and temples were built and rebuilt on the site. The Menelaion remained an important religious centre even after classical Sparta arose on the opposite bank. However, in Spartan times the personages worshipped on the Menelaion had changed from the former gods and were now heroes who had lived in the Bronze Age. (Including the Homeric King Menelaus, for whom the site is now named.)

In terms of the overall geopolitics of Bronze Age Greece, the Menelaion was a significant city. It was probably in the second rank though, behind the great centres of Mycenae, Thebes and recently-formed Athens. Indeed, much of Greece itself was something of a backwater in comparison to the thriving centres of civilization in Egypt, Mesopotamia and the Aegean Islands. Given the military outlook of the Mycenaean Greeks, it is perhaps unsurprising their most outstanding feat of the late Bronze Age was the collective effort which destroyed the city of Ilium on the western coast of Asia Minor.

While this attack is famed in myth as the 'siege of Troy', little is known of the actual history of that event. In fact it was only around 150 years ago that Troy was discovered to have been a real city, and subsequent archaeology revealed it to have been destroyed more or less at the time that the legends said it had been, that is, at around 1250 BC.

Soon after this, something happened. Not just to Greece, but to the entire civilized world of the eastern Mediterranean. The exact cause is unknown, but whatever took place at the end of the thirteenth century was truly catastrophic. One theory is that Thera blew up yet again. The island of Santorini is today a circular ring with a huge sea-filled hole where the caldera of Thera has erupted, not once but several times, and at least once with a force greater than Krakatoa, the most powerful volcanic explosion of modern times. Whereas Krakatoa was a relatively remote island in the Pacific, Thera had not one, but several civilizations close by.

A major volcanic eruption in the eastern Mediterranean would have been immediately and immensely catastrophic. Certainly this would have been enough to end the Bronze Age all by itself. However climate change, especially drought, a major plague, or a combination of all of the above have also been suggested as trigger factors for the disaster which almost obliterated civilisation in the region. The problem with so major a cataclysm was that there were few left to write about it, and little chance of the record surviving if someone had done so. Consequently, the cause of the Bronze Age remains as mysterious as it was comprehensively destructive.

The Hittite empire in Anatolia fell, and Syria collapsed into ruin. The once-magnificent Minoan civilization on Crete vanished almost completely. Even Egypt, where civilization had been established for thousands of years, was not immune. The country suffered massive internal turmoil and invasion from abroad, and even that mighty civilization almost went under.

Mycenaean Greece was basically wiped out. Archaeology shows that almost all the major population centres were destroyed, while lesser ones were simply abandoned. Pottery, always a good indicator of a society's sophistication, went from elegantly painted vases to crude blobs of clay. Writing was essentially forgotten, so the written record disappears for several centuries before writing was reinvented. When writing did reappear, it was in a totally different form with no connection to the past. Overall, Greece plunged into a dark age that lasted until the early eighth century. For around 300 years we have almost no record of what happened in Greece as a whole, let alone in the corner of Laconia that was to become Sparta.

We do know that at some point around 1000 BC it appears that two villages grew up near the remains of the Menelaion, but on the other side of the River Eurotas. Common sense in troubled times suggested that the two villages should share the effort of fortifying the nearest hillock into an acropolis (literally 'high city') as a place of refuge in an emergency. Combined effort seems to have led eventually to combined villages. (It may be from the leaders of these two villages that the later tradition of Sparta having two kings originated.) From this obscure beginning Sparta was born. The peoples of these two combined villages were not, however, the inhabitants of Menelaion who had rehoused themselves across the river. What became of those original inhabitants is unknown, but Laconia was now occupied by a different people, the Dorians.

The Dorians were from the north, probably from the Balkans. As with most things of Dark Age Greece, what we know of the arrival of the Dorians is obscure and speculative. Even the term for their arrival – the 'Dorian invasion' – may be a misnomer for a people who may have simply taken vacant possession of abandoned sites. Some historians have suggested that the Dorians were always present in the Peloponnese as a subject population, rather as the helots were later to be in Sparta. When the collapse came, the Dorians overthrew their masters and took over. Whatever their origins, by the end of the Dark Age the Dorians were masters of the Peloponnese including Laconia, and the Spartans of the classical era proudly identified themselves as being Doric. (Apart from their kings, for reasons we shall come to later.)

As ever, destruction engendered creation. Before the Dark Age, elaborate trade routes had been essential for civilization. These trade routes collapsed along with the rest of Bronze Age civilization. Without tin (by some accounts from as far away as Britain) copper could not be forged into bronze, and tin was relatively rare. Without this key metal, the alloy that gave the Bronze Age its name fell into disuse. Presumably out of desperation, someone in Anatolia experimented with smelting iron ore, and discovered that iron – once a metal rarer than gold – could be extracted from certain reddish-looking soils. Even more remarkable, carbon released by the charcoal in the forging process could be taken up by the red-hot iron to create steel. True, the process was somewhat hit-and-miss, but when all worked well, swords stronger and more flexible than anything wielded by the Mycenaean kings became widely available. As a result, the people of Greece emerged from the Dark Age even better-armed and ferociously warlike than they had gone into it. This went double for the Spartans, for their location in one of the most fertile areas of the Eurotas valley meant that they had the population and resources to dedicate to warfare which less fortunate folks had to dedicate to simple survival.

Seafaring also had greatly developed during the latter part

of the Dark Age. The Phoenicians, a Semitic people from the Levant, were early adopters of the improved technology, and were instrumental in re-establishing Mediterranean trade routes. For a while they established a settlement on inhospitable Cape Malea for the processing of dyes. The Greeks quickly followed the Phoenician example and turned to the sea, quickly becoming accomplished traders and settling trading posts that rapidly became colonies around the shores of the Mediterranean.

By the time the historical record had become re-established, the Greeks were spread far and wide. The Dorians of Sparta could claim kinship with Dorian Syracuse, Rhodes, and even Cyrene in Africa. Even the Spartans themselves, never the most aquatically-minded of the Greeks, had founded a few colonies of their own, most notably on the little island of Melos. They had even established a colony on Thera, on the remains of the volcano that might have started the whole disaster.

So, as Greece stumbled toward recovery in the ninth century, Sparta was as it had been in the previous era. Though renamed and relocated on the other side of the Eurotas, Sparta was again a Greek city of the second rank, dominant locally but something of a backwater in the wider world of Greek civilization. In culture, size and traditions, Sparta entered the classical era as a perfectly average city.

That was about to change.

Origins part II. Sex and Violence

A Spartan of the classical era would have read the above account and rejected it with angry incredulity. One purpose of history is to give a community its identity. It does this by telling the people who they are, where they came from and what they have done. Consequently the Spartans had no need of the historical record given above. The Spartans had already given themselves a clear narrative which told them who they were and where they came from.

Since the Spartans firmly believed their own narrative, that was the story which shaped their concept of themselves. Modern historians may deride it as a mixture of myth, distorted memory and outright self-serving invention, but that was the narrative which shaped the Spartan mind-set and made the community into the people and society who they were. Therefore in many ways, the story that the Spartans believed is more important than the story of what 'actually' happened. The Spartan story of their origins had several versions, depending on who was doing the telling and why, but the basic plot is essentially the same.

So let us begin again, and retell the story of Sparta's origins with a synthesis of the different legends which, according to the Spartans, is how their land and people really came about.

After the world was destroyed by the great flood which ended the Age of Bronze, the Heroic Age began (very approximately in 1300 BC). In the restored world, the first settlers in Laconia were the people of one King Lelex, the grandson of whom was called Eurotas. Eurotas became king in his turn, and drained the marshy valley of central Laconia by digging a ditch to the sea. This ditch remained and widened over the years to become the Eurotas River. However, unlike the banks of the river he created, King Eurotas was infertile. Childless, he had to look outside his family for an heir.

The chosen one was a man called Lacedaemon, though there was little of 'man' in his hereditary. The father of Lacedaemon was a Titan, one of the primordial species from the earliest times of the world. Nor was the father just any Titan, but Zeus himself, King of the Gods. Though a married man, Zeus had a weakness for seducing nymphs. One such nymph was Taygete, a daughter of Atlas, that Titan whom Zeus had given the task of holding up the heavens. Being nature deities, nymphs were usually associated with a particular stream, wood or mountain. With Taygete, her chosen haunt was a mountain overlooking the newly-formed Eurotas River, which mountain later took her name – Mount Taygetus. Here on Mount Taygetus the nymph Taygete was 'seduced' (read 'raped') by Zeus, and in due course she bore a son. This was Lacedaemon, who was thus mostly Titan by his father and maternal grandfather, but in no ways human.

In order to bring this remarkable personage into his family, Eurotas married Lacedaemon to his daughter, a charming princess called Sparta. Just as the near-contemporary Greek hero Pelops ruled the land so effectively that it eventually took his name and became the Peloponnese, Lacedaemon's little kingdom became Lacadaemonia. The principal town took its name from the royal bride and became Sparta. (Though we note that, since classical Sparta was still meadowland, the Sparta of myth must have been the settlement of the Menelaion.)

We now fast-forward through three generations to Tyndareus, a grandson (on his mother's side) of Perseus, the hero who slew the Gorgon Medusa. Tyndareus fell out with his brother over the kingship and retired in exile to Pellana. (We note how this echoes the suggestion of rivalry between Pellana and Sparta in the historical Bronze Age.) While in exile, Tyndareus found a mighty ally and relative in another descendant of Perseus. This was none other than Hercules, who for reasons we need not go into here, had a grudge against the current king of Sparta. It is a little-known fact that, as well as slaying assorted monsters in his renowned Labours, Hercules in his spare time was a war leader who brought sudden death to many monarchs in southern Greece. He slew at least half a dozen of them, including the unfortunate king of Sparta.

The Spartan throne now belonged to Hercules by right of conquest, but the mighty hero had not the time to rule a relatively obscure corner of south-eastern Greece. Instead Hercules appointed Tyndareus as a sort of regent, to rule Laconia in place of Hercules until the hero, or his descendants, returned to claim the throne.

'King' Tyndareus settled down to rule his new kingdom, and took as a wife the beautiful Leda, a princess of Aetolia. All then proceeded smoothly until that fateful afternoon when Leda beheld a swan in distress from being attacked by an eagle. Leda succoured the swan, unaware that both swan and eagle were part of a cunning plan by which Zeus intended to get under Leda's chiton. As matters progressed it became clear that Leda was prepared to go along with events as her swan became a swain and went from victim to seducer. The resultant amorous bout has inspired artists through the ages, from medieval woodcuts to Leonardo da Vinci and some remarkably pornographic efforts in the nineteenth century.

Leda's adventure with cygnophilia was followed by the more standard form of sex that night with Tyndareus. The remarkable upshot of the whole business was that Leda later gave birth to a pair of eggs. Each egg contained a mortal and a divine child, these being the children of Zeus and Tyndareus respectively. The first egg in the clutch contained the divine Castor, and the mortal Pollux. Pollux became deified later, and one-twelfth of the world's population have reason to celebrate the pair, who are currently enshrined in the heavens as the sign of Gemini ('the twins'). The second egg was even more remarkable, for it contained the mortal Clytemnestra, who was to become the wife – and killer – of Agamemnon of Mycenae. The second occupant of this egg was the divine Helen, the most beautiful woman who ever lived.

Uncanny beauty such as Helen's rested uneasily in a world of mortals. That this beauty was to become a cause of strife became clear even before Helen entered puberty. Two kings, Peirithous of Larissa and Theseus of Athens, were visiting Sparta when they beheld Helen dancing at the temple of Artemis Orthia. (Archaeologists think they may have found the remains of this temple on the Menelaion.) Both kings instantly desired to possess Helen, for all that she was still a child. An impulsive kidnap was followed by a desperate chase across the Peloponnese as Theseus and Peirithous fled with their captive.

On reaching safety near Argos, the detestable pair drew straws to decide who was to have Helen. Theseus won, whereupon Peirithous declared he must have for himself another daughter of Zeus. They decided that, if Theseus was to have Helen, then Peirithous would rape Persephone, daughter of Zeus by Demeter, the Corn Goddess. Persephone had married Hades, King of the Underworld, but the two dastardly adventurers seem to have given little thought to the perils which such an enterprise involved. Therefore, after stashing Helen with the mother of Theseus in a town outside Athens, the pair set off for the kingdom of Hades on their madcap adventure.

While Theseus was away getting Persephone (the attempt did not end well), Castor and Pollux arrived at Athens with a Spartan army. They requested the return of Helen, initially politely, and then with increasing vehemence. Matters deteriorated to the point where the Spartans first defeated the Athenians in war and then proceeded to ransack Attica looking for their missing princess. Finally, one Academus correctly decided that there was no reason why the entire state should suffer to protect an absent child-rapist, and he revealed Helen's whereabouts to the Spartans. (Which is why, centuries later in the Peloponnesian War, the Spartans regularly devastated the lands of Attica but left untouched the property of the heirs of Academus.)

Since Theseus was deemed to have brought Helen to womanhood, on the return of Helen to Sparta the city was promptly besieged by a swarm of suitors hoping to marry her. Helen eventually settled on Menelaus, a prince of Mycenae, and thereafter Tyndareus and Leda resigned to allow the pair to rule Laconia in their stead. Then along came Paris of Troy.

The kidnap of Helen led to the famous ten-year siege which ended with the destruction of Troy. This siege taught later generations of classical Spartans several things about themselves. Firstly, that they were a people who were very touchy on matters of honour. (Compare the Spartan reaction to the kidnap of Helen with the more insouciant comment of the historian Herodotus: 'It is silly to make a fuss about the kidnap of a woman, for it is clear that no woman is taken who does not want to go.')

Furthermore, the Spartans had now established in their tradition that not only were they entitled to invade peoples who had aggrieved them, but that they expected to win the subsequent war. Finally, the interest taken by gods and men in the people and affairs of Laconia proved to the Spartans not just that they mattered in the affairs of Greece, but they were a people who took a decisive role in sorting out those affairs. A proud nation then, prepared to become as violent as necessary to obtain satisfaction if offended. Certainly later Greeks would have recognized this description of the Spartans.

For the next two generations after the fall of Troy, it was business as usual in the mythical Peloponnese. That is to say there were a few minor but vicious wars, the family of Tyndareus and descendants had complex soap-opera style lives and the gods kept interfering. Then, at around the time of the end of the Bronze Age in the archaeological record, the Peloponnese of legend was invaded and occupied by a people from the north. This invasion and occupation is recorded both by archaeology and tradition, though Spartan tradition would certainly not admit anything as demeaning as the conquest of Laconia by a foreign tribe, even if – especially if – the later Spartans *were* that foreign tribe.

No, in their tradition the Spartans remained the descendants of Zeus and Taygete, the people of Helen. Their leadership was merely taken over by the great-grandsons of Hercules – and Hercules, it will be recalled, had a legitimate claim to the kingship of the place. The sons of Hercules (numerous enough in themselves) had been exiled to the north until the still more numerous 'third crop' – ie the third generation – returned to the Peloponnese to claim their inheritance, just as the Oracle at Delphi had prophesied.

Thus, rather than foreign invaders, the new rulers of the Peloponnese were actually native sons of the region, for their ancestor Hercules was born in Achaea, not far from Mycenae. This is why, in the Classical era, when a king of Sparta was ordered from an Athenian temple because he was a Dorian, the King politely told the priestess, 'No, ma'am. I am Achaean.' (Politely, because Spartan men were more respectful of women than other contemporary Greeks.) The distinction between Dorians and the descendants of Hercules was politely fudged over for the general population of Spartiates, who insisted that they were both Doric and descendants of Taygete.

There were two claimants to the kingship of Laconia – the twin brothers Procles and Eurysthenes. Since the mother was unable to remember which twin had been born first, she consulted the Oracle at Delphi as to which son was entitled to the throne. The Oracle told her that both sons should rule, thus creating the unique joint kingship which became a feature of the Spartan system thereafter.

Neighbouring Messenia was allotted to another descendant of Hercules called Cresphontes – literally 'allotted' because the twins and Cresphontes drew lots for the region. Messenia was actually considered a better prize than Laconia, for the region was more fertile, prosperous and populous. It was agreed that contenders for the rule of this rich kingdom would draw wooden lots by elimination from a vase filled with water. The lots with the names of Procles and Eurysthenes floated out first, so the twins were eliminated and Cresphontes became the winner by default. This outcome was later revealed to have come about because Cresphontes had cheated. Rather than use a strip of wood, he had fashioned his lot from mud. This dissolved away in the water of the vase and could never emerge. (For his sins Cresphontes was later murdered by the ungrateful Messenians.)

From this story the Spartans took the message that Messenia legitimately belonged to the Laconian kings who had been cheated of their possession. As a people who obtained their satisfaction for wrongs by physical force, it was obviously up to the Spartan army to restore Messania to its 'rightful rulers'. This in the end is exactly what the Spartans did.

Chapter Two

Becoming Sparta

I. The Wider World

Sparta may have been preoccupied with gaining control of the Eurotas valley while being both covetous and fearful of the more fertile lands and greater population of Messenia, but both Spartans and Messenians were aware that they were also peoples of the newly-arisen land of Hellas.

As their name for themselves suggests, the Greeks ('Hellenes') still saw themselves as the people of Helle, son of the mythical Deculion who was one of the first humans to occupy Greece after the mythical flood which had destroyed the previous occupants. However, like the landscape after that flood, the Greece which emerged after the Dark Age was radically different from the land which had gone before. The old centres of power were gone, replaced by new political entities. Foremost of these entities was the *polis*, the city-state. (From where we get words such as 'politician' and 'polite', as opposed to rural uncouthness.)

In Bronze Age Greece, the political landscape had been dominated by kingdoms centred on relatively large cities such as Mycenae. The rulers of these kingdoms exercised power over their own states and also over subordinate kings. As we have seen in the apparent tension between Pallene and the Menelaion, the capital of one of these ancient kingdoms was where the king wanted it to be. Political power was based on the king, not on his whereabouts.

In the new Greece of the Archaic era, this had changed. Now the centre of power was the *polis*, and a ruler without his *polis* was merely a powerless exile. (And the ruler was unlikely to be a king. The *poleis* were experimenting with different governmental forms, including oligarchies of rich aristocrats and autocratic tyrants who ruled as kings but without the legitimacy of an inherited crown.)

Among the new centres of power were the city-states of Athens and Corinth. Athens was a particularly large city-state, as the different towns and villages of Attica in western Greece had been united into a single political entity – according to legend by Theseus, our child-abducting king of the Heroic Age of myth. Next to Athens was the land of Boeotia, renowned for its beautiful women and allegedly slow-thinking males. The principal city was Thebes, which with its highly-defensible acropolis, had also been a centre of power during the Bronze Age. Next came Corinth, a city which was fabulously rich, as it was situated on the isthmus which connected the Peloponnese with the rest of Greece. From this strategic location Corinth benefited both from sea trade which was hauled across the narrow isthmus, and from land traffic moving from north to south.

In the Peloponnese, to the south-east of Corinth lay a fertile and long-settled area called the Argolid, which was situated between rocky Arcadia and the sea. Just south of ancient Mycenae, and nearer the coast as befitted the seafaring nature of the Greeks of the new era was the new principal city of the Argolid; the *polis* of Argos. At the start of the Archaic era Argos was probably the leading city of the Peloponnese, a status which Sparta, hemmed in by the confines of the Eurotas valley, could only envy. The Spartans were well aware that theirs was a second-rank city, for even their expansion into the lands at the Eurotas headwaters gave room for only modest population growth. Expansion yet further north was blocked by Argos itself, so if Sparta was to grow beyond the confines of Laconia, the only direction was west, into Messenia.

Messenia was not a *polis*, for though there came to be a city of Messenia, this was founded late in the Classical Era. Rather the Messenians formed what the Greeks considered an *ethnos* – a tribe. 'Tribe' in this sense does not carry the connotations of unsophisticated barbarism with which later ages have burdened the word. In many ways an *ethnos* as a political entity was more sophisticated than a *polis*. In an *ethnos* no single city was dominant, and the member states formed a rough confederation which, no matter how vicious the political infighting, usually presented a united front to the outside world. (Dorians and Achaeans were also *ethne*, and though the Dorians were slow to confederate, in later years the Achaeans were to form a very effective federation.) Early federations existed in Thessaly to the north, in Aetolia in the north-west, in Arcadia, and of course in Messenia.

To the north of the Greek peninsula was a kingdom in the standard sense – a large state centred on a king. This was Macedonia, which the Hellenes regarded as too backward and primitive to be properly Greek, no matter how much the Macedonian kings objected to this designation.

Of course, there was much more to Greece in the Archaic and Classical Eras than just mainland Greece. Some of the most important and dynamic centres of Hellenic civilization were overseas, in Sicily, Crete, on mainland Anatolia and on the islands between. Here was found Mytilene on the island of Lesbos, where later Alcaeus was to become one of Greece's most famous lyric poets, outmatched perhaps only by another fellow-citizen – Sappho, whom Plato called 'the tenth muse'. Yet Mytilene was just one example of the brilliant culture of Ionia, as the Greek cities of Anatolia and the Aegean Islands were collectively known. Other Ionian cities such as Miletus and Ephesus were to be early pathfinders in the fifth-century intellectual revolution which was famously taken over by Athens in a burst of discovery that has in its turn laid the foundations for our modern era.

That Athens should have become the centre for Ionian culture is unsurprising, for Athens also identified as Ionian. The original Ionians, according to their own tradition, came from the Peloponnese. The ancient Greeks also wondered what became of the peoples displaced by the Dorians in Sparta and elsewhere, and their belief was the refugees had fled east to the Aegean islands and the Anatolian seaboard. This is a somewhat simplistic explanation, as archaeology has shown that some Ionian cities already existed in the Bronze Age, but it was what the Greeks believed, and their belief became of major political importance when Doric Sparta eventually faced Ionian Athens in war.

The origins of most Greek colonies are obscure, because most of them were already in place by the time the chaos of the Dark Age cleared enough for anyone to start keeping proper records again. Most of these new cities had at least a tradition of where their colonists had come from, but origins did not equal political control. Greek colonies might feel a sentimental fondness for their 'mother-city' but they no more took orders from that mother city than, say, modern Australia does from the British government. While Ionians and Dorians might have their own festivals, religious centres and traditions, the fiercely independent and warlike cities of the new Greece were quite happy to ally with whomever might give them an advantage over the neighbours, be they Ionian, Dorian or Achaean.

Thus, for example, in Sicily a Greek *polis* might easily find itself engaged in a three-way fight with the native Sicels, a nearby rival city and against the Carthaginians who had also colonised the island. Likewise, a city which had been an ally in a previous war might just as easily be an enemy in the present one. Alliances were fluid and changed with the political situation. (Though one constant in Sicilian politics was that Greeks and Carthaginians loathed each other so passionately that they almost never collaborated.)

Just as the Greeks of the Aegean Islands and Anatolia are known as the Ionians, the colonies to the west of Greece itself are usually called 'Magna Graecia'. They were a diverse bunch, from the 'New City' on the west of the Italian peninsula ('Nea Polis' in Greek, 'Neapoli' in modern Italian, 'Naples' in English) to Cyrene on the African coast, and Emporiai nestled against the Pyrenees in Iberia.

Even to land-locked Sparta deep in the Peloponnese, these overseas cities mattered. The Greeks were now a seafaring and trading people, and goods flowed readily from Asia Minor, the Crimea and Egypt (where the Greeks had a trading post) through Greece to Southern Italy and back. With the movement of people and goods went the movement of ideas. A good example of this is the alphabet, which as far as can be ascertained, developed in Egypt among mercenary troops stationed there. Instead of using the pictograms of hieroglyphic-style writing, these soldiers used letters to represent parts of speech. The idea was quickly adopted by the Phoenicians (including the Carthaginians, who were colonists from Phoenicia). The Greeks took the idea from the Phoenicians and turned the letters sideways, removing the last pictographic elements. Thus the little horned head representing 'aelph' the bull, became the meaningless 'alpha' of Greek and the 'a' of the modern alphabet. The Greek script was picked up by Italian peoples, including the Etruscans, who later passed it to the Romans, who adapted it further and passed it to posterity.

While later Spartans tended to regard new ideas with suspicion, and trade as sapping the native industry and honesty of a people, archaic Sparta was little different from other Greek cities. The early Spartans shared in, and contributed to, the common myths, poems, dances and songs that spread and united the extended Hellenic world.

While Sparta shared in the movement of ideas, the city was disadvantaged in the movement of goods. The city was situated in the most fertile part of the Eurotas valley, and this part was inland from the sea. Even the mouth of the Eurotas River was not easily accessible by merchantmen, because getting there involved negotiating the hazards of at least one of the three rocky peninsulas that stretched southward from the main body of the Peloponnese. The optimal sea route would have been from the east, since most of the trading centres of Archaic and Classical Greece lay in that direction. But the sea route between Sparta and points east was blocked by the rocky peninsula which ended at Cape Malea – and Cape Malea was infamous in the ancient Mediterranean for storms and shipwreck.

Thus Sparta's rivals – Athens, Argos and particularly Corinth – became rich from trade. Indeed, even distant Sybaris in Italy became so rich that still today 'sybaritic' is an adjective for luxurious decadence. Sparta, meanwhile had to make do with the scraps from this particular table. Geography had ensured that Sparta could never be a trading nation, and geology – in the form of confining, barren mountain ranges – had ensured that Sparta could not grow through agriculture, mining or industry. Sparta could only fight its way out of this particular box, and thus became a military power through necessity. At the same time the city made a virtue of doing without the things it couldn't get anyway. Not by co-incidence does 'Spartan' have the opposite meaning to 'Sybaritic'.

II. Birth of a Warrior Nation

While the Spartan legend is reasonably clear on the subject, and we are sure that Sparta came to consciously identify itself as Dorian in dialect and custom, ethnologists today are actually unsure who the Dorians were, how many they numbered or their relationship with the original Achaeans. The classical narrative clearly demarcates the two ethnic groups, but the question is moot whether the difference was one of ancestral origin or self-identification by peoples struggling back from the chaos of the Dark Age which followed the fall of Mycenaean Greece.

In the Eurotas Valley the fall was so deep and total that it appears only one settlement remained continuously inhabited – Amyklai, the former satellite village of the Menelaion. As recovery began from the ravages of the Dark Age, it was natural that one of the first areas to begin that recovery would be the agriculturally fertile and defensively secure area around the (now destroyed) Menelaoin. Four villages grew up on the west bank of the River Eurotas; Pitana and Mesoa, Limnai and Konoura. It is credibly postulated that Pitana and Mesoa were the first of these villages, and these gradually confederated because of the necessity of jointly maintaining their acropolis as a fortress of last refuge. With an expanding population, Limnai and Konoura developed soon afterwards.

Whatever their actual origins, the population of these four villages consciously identified as Dorian. This mattered because the Dorians had a 'warp and woof' structure which wove tribe and community together. All archaic Greek communities were led by a king, and below him, by a small group of warrior aristocrats who in peacetime served the state as administrators and judges. Among the Spartans, each of these aristocrats was leader of an aristocratic faction (*phratry*), comprising his own family, subordinate households, including those of subordinate families, and the lands, slaves and other assets controlled by that faction. Members of a faction were educated together, and shared many common facilities. Each king and faction was local, and these comprised the 'warp' of the Dorian people's social fabric.

The 'woof' was made from three tribes, Hylleis, Pamphyli and Dymanes. Dorians everywhere belonged to one of these tribes, and were expected to favour and assist fellow tribesmen above other Dorians as a whole, and certainly above other Greeks in general. Thus every Dorian owed allegiance to Dorians outside his own community, but also to his own faction and king. We see this dual social structure in the arrangement of the Spartans at war, when the Spartan army was led by a king, Spartan regiments were organized by tribe, and the subdivisions of the regiments were based on the faction. (The Spartans were unique in having not one king but two, enabling one king to remain at home looking after domestic administration while the other went to war.)

Theoretically these two kings were the descendants of the twins who originally ruled Sparta – Procles and Eurysthenes – the pair who lost Messenia to Cresphontes in the crooked lottery. In practice it seems clear that the original kings were the 'Agiad' line. If their traditional burial place near the village of Pitana is any indication, these Agiad kings represented the original leaders of the merged communities of Pitana and Mesoa. By the time Limnai and Konoura joined the confederation they too were united under one line of kings, the 'Eurypontids'. These two royal families – Agiads and Eurypontids – ruled jointly for most of Spartan history.

If we are to believe the Spartan king lists, in early Sparta each king was the son of his predecessor, a pattern of succession which went in an unbroken line right back to either Agis or Eurypontus, the children of Procles and Eurysthenes. Given that the later succession in better-recorded historical times is much messier, it is clear that the early lists were dramatically edited and adjusted to make the chronology of succession fit with other recorded events. Thus the list of early kings has the same relationship with reality as does the rest of early Sparta's foundation legend – that is, legend and reality meet awkwardly at irregular intervals to give birth to another generation of myths which bear a strong resemblance to reality.

Given the presence of the well-established settlement of Amyklai just a few kilometres south of newly confederated Sparta, it is unsurprising that the city's first attempts at expansion were away from Amyklai, to the north. Under successive kings progress was made in subjugating minor settlements around the headwaters of the Eurotas River until the northern part of Laconia fell more or less under the Spartan hegemony. Turning southward, the Spartans then absorbed such minor communities as stood between themselves and Amyklai, and finally took over

Amyklai itself. While most of the hamlets facing absorption by the Spartan state decided that resistance was useless, Amyklai fought hard and was only taken after a bitter siege. With that bulwark against expansion removed, Sparta went on to dominate the remainder of the Eurotas valley, and thus all of Laconia.

Places such as Amyklai were close enough to be made part of Sparta itself. However, the absorption of Amyklai as a place did not include the absorption of the population of Amyklai, which was re-settled by members of the expanding Spartiate community. Some idea of what happened to the original inhabitants might be drawn from the fate of the people of nearby Helos. These people were made slaves, not of individual Spartan conquerors, but possessions of the Spartan state itself, allotted to work in the fields of various Spartan landowners as the government saw fit. Most classical Greeks with an interest in etymology assumed that the people of Helos supplied the original name later given to all of Sparta's semi-slave population, the helots. However, later researchers note that the word has the '*hel-*' root which means 'captured' or 'subjugated'.

Dominance did not, apart from those villages in immediate proximity to Sparta, necessarily mean absorption and slavery. Those settlements which did not become part of the 'city' of Sparta itself generally remained autonomous administrative units. The peoples of these outer settlements became the *perioiki*. They had to contribute to Sparta's efforts both financially and by adding their manpower to the Spartan army, but to a certain extent they could consider themselves independent peoples. This did not stop Sparta's magistrates from interfering in the affairs of the *perioiki* as they felt necessary, or even on occasion putting *perioiki* to death without trial. Consequently other Greeks tended to see Laconia as a single state, and its people as the Lacedaemonians, but in reality there was a real separation.

Perhaps a workable analogy might be drawn from the twentieth century. If the USA was rather like Attica, which region had become a single city under Athens, Laconia was more like the former USSR. Outsiders tended to refer to the people of the USSR as 'Russians' despite the very real differences which were revealed when the USSR broke up.

At this point we are still operating in the twilight zone

where the scraps unearthed by archaeology and the unreliable traditions of the Spartans and their enemies give us only uncertain glimpses into early Spartan history. Thus we note that according to Spartan tradition, a King Teleclus dispatched three groups of colonists to settle in Messenian territory on the other side of the Taygetos Range. Teleclus himself was later killed by the Messenians in highly controversial circumstances which will be described at length below.

II. The Contentious Messenian Narrative

Sometime in the late eighth century BC Sparta invaded the neighbouring region of Messenia. That much is certain. Almost everything else about this momentous event is not. It is precisely because this conquest so dramatically and completely shaped later Spartan history that it is hard to get the exact details. Sparta's occupation of Messenia came to define the Spartan state, so the Spartans tried hard to persuade both themselves and others that this occupation was justified. This required a special effort, as no other Greek state in the classical era ever took over a neighbour in this way. The truth was one of the first casualties of the Spartan effort, and even the historian Pausanias, writing in the Roman era, complains bitterly of the paucity and unreliability of his sources.

Since Pausanias seems to have made a conscientious effort to establish what happened, and because almost all other accounts are lost, it is largely on Pausanias that our account of the origins of the war must perforce be based. However, we note these caveats which the frustrated historian has scattered through his introduction.

'Most matters of Greek history have come to be disputed. ... If Pindar is to be believed, the eyesight of Lynceus the younger was so sharp that he saw through the trunk of an oak tree. ... Neither writer [Myron nor Rhianus] managed a complete and continuous account of the whole war from its beginning to the end, but each chose to describe only of a part of it. As their statements differ so widely, I have been forced to adopt one or other of their narratives, but not both together. ... By looking at the rest of his work, one realizes that Myron is blithely heedless of the fact that his statements appear to lack truth and credibility, and this is particularly so in his Messenian history.'

Pausanias *Guide to Greece* 4.2-6

In short what remained of the history of the Messenian conflict was preserved not by sober historians, but by propagandists, poets and myth-mongers. We cannot be too shocked by this, as History as a craft developed centuries later than the Messenian invasion. Even then, as one of the first historians – Thucydides of Athens – was to discover, the Spartans actively discouraged those who dug too deeply into the details of their past.

Given Sparta's efforts to control the narrative, it is no surprise to discover that the earliest records of Messenia suggest that at the time of the Trojan War the region was under Laconian control. The 'Catalogue of Ships' in Homer's Iliad seems to agree. Homer (or a source which has been inserted into the Homeric epic) lists all the ships of the Greek army, who commanded them, and where they were from. The ships of the southern Peloponnese all have the same (Laconian) commander, whether they were from Messenia or Laconia. The geographer Strabo, writing in the Roman era, draws the unambiguous conclusion about Messenia, 'This country was part of Laconia.' (Strabo *Geography* 8.4.1)

Strabo's opinion would have suited the Spartans well. If it could be established that Messenia was a dependency of Laconia even before the Dorian invasion, then the Spartan occupation of their neighbours' land could be presented as a return to the status quo rather than a disturbing new development. 'Disturbing' because, apart from Sparta, even if they conquered it, the classical Greeks never permanently occupied the territory of another state, let alone enslaved the inhabitants. At most, other Greeks might replace the original inhabitants of a defeated city with their own colonists, but those colonists quickly became independent entities in their own right. To justify their invasion and subsequent actions, the Spartans needed to show, firstly, that Laconian rule of Messenia was rooted in historical precedent, and secondly that an independent Messenia was an existential threat to Sparta.

The story of the time of Messenian independence between the Dorian invasion and Spartan conquest is therefore one of competing narratives. The Spartans' narrative attempts to defend their invasion and justify the subsequent occupation of Messenia. Sparta's rivals – and the Messenians themselves – attempted to portray Sparta's actions as perfidious, unjustified and unjust. The overall story which emerges from this dialectic is almost certainly more fiction than fact, but it is worth retelling, firstly because it is all we have, and secondly because it shaped how Sparta was perceived by others and also shaped how the Spartans perceived themselves.

Immediately after the Dorian invasion Strabo tells us that when the Heraclid Cresphontes took over Messenia, he divided the region into five administrative centres each based on a city. This is reasonable enough because the region's geography is indeed amenable to such a division. The capital city was called Stenyclerus, and it was there that most of the Dorian population made their home. We have seen that King Cresphontes came to an untimely end when he attempted to force Dorian dominance over the Achaean Messenians. In response, the Achaeans overthrew Cresphontes and killed him.

Thus the basic cause of the Messenian war as given by the poets is credible enough. That is, this was a war which had at its root that unfailing wellspring of conflict – ethnic tension; in this case between the Dorian newcomers and the original Achaean inhabitants of the Southern Peloponnese.

While Cresphontes was alive, the Spartan leaders were none too impressed with him as a person, but the Spartans were well aware that the precedent of Achaeans overthrowing their Dorian overlords could not be allowed to stand. After all, the Spartans also were Dorians with a large proportion of Achaean subjects. Accordingly, a Spartan army marched over the passes of the Taygetos Range and restored the Dorians to power.

Cresphontes being deceased, the Laconians might have considered putting one of their own into the kingship. Instead, they chose to restore the son of Cresphontes to his father's throne. This son was called Aepytus. Aepytus was determined to avoid his father's fate. He was well aware that, given the difficulties of communication over the mountain passes, Sparta may avenge him in the event of another uprising, but Sparta could not save him or prevent such an uprising happening in the first place.

Therefore Aepytus threw himself into seducing his Achaean subjects into acceptance of his rule. Indeed, the very name by which we know this man, Aepytus, may have been taken from Messenian city of Aepy. By thus identifying himself with the country (rather as the post-Hanoverian British royal family did by taking the name of Windsor), the king and his later successors strongly downplayed their origins and concentrated on being more native than the natives.

In Messenia this worked to the extent that the Achaeans began to consider the Aepytid dynasty as their legitimate leaders. Naturally enough, the Dorian population of Messenia did not share their rulers' delight at this outcome. Instead of being a conquering elite, the Messenian Dorians felt marginalized and unwanted. They looked increasingly to Sparta for support and protection, and Sparta readily gave this, for Sparta had taken the opposite direction. Over the years Sparta increasingly identified as Dorian to the extent that the Achaean population gradually lost even their membership of the state and became (by this interpretation of events) the *perioiki* of Laconia.

Given goodwill on both sides, there was no reason why Achaean Messenia and Dorian Sparta could not have lived amicably side by side, as they did at the start of the eighth century. Good fences, they say, make good neighbours, and the Taygetos Range was more than sufficient to separate the two nations.

The range is not shaped like a stereotypical mountain, with triangular sides sloping up to a central peak. Rather it resembles an extremely lumpy table tilted to one side. There is a (relatively) gentle slope tilting toward Messenia and on the Spartan side, a practically sheer drop into the Eurotas Valley. Nor is the range a geographical whole. The northern section extends into Arcadia, and is extremely rough and in places impassable. The southern massif, the Dentheliatis, is more hospitable, so much so that the Romans used the name 'the Dentheliathian fields' to somewhat optimistically describe the amount of arable land between the peaks. This area was more suitable for the movement of traders or armies, and the Dentheliatis region was the nexus of communications between Laconia, Messenia and Arcadia.

It was of the highest importance that it be clearly demarcated which parts of the Dentheliatis were controlled by Sparta, and which fell under Messenian jurisdiction. Consequently, there arose, right on the border, a temple and sanctuary. This was dedicated to the Goddess who was patron of the entire Taygetos Range (and in myth, also the patron of the nymph Taygete herself) – Artemis, the Goddess of the Hunt. Her temple at this diplomatically sensitive location was dedicated to Artemis Limnatis. 'Artemis of the rushing waters.' Later archaeology has tentatively placed this temple near the modern village of Pigadhia, in a steep valley which curves south-west into Messenia.

Here at the temple Messenians and Laconians interacted, and indeed even took part in joint religious celebrations. At this point, in the mid-eighth century, relations between the two nations were quite amicable. However, at one such celebration something went horribly wrong. Both Laconians and Messenians agreed that the perfidious actions of one of the nations at the celebration were so vile that they engendered an enduring legacy of hatred which thereafter lasted as long as did the Messenians and Spartans themselves. Pausanias tells the story in his *Guide to Greece* (4.4.2), which story is summarized below.

It appears that Teleclus, (the colonizing Spartan king whom we have already met above) took a group of young maidens to the temple of Artemis Limnatis to celebrate a religious festival. On arrival they found that the temple was already occupied by a large number of young Messenian men who were there either for the same festival or for a different celebration. In either case, some religious festivals in ancient Greece had much in common with the religious festivals of Christmas and Easter in the West today. That is, socializing and parties played a major role apart from the actual religious event. We might perhaps imagine a raucous party of young men who had got well into their wine cups when suddenly a group of young women turned up. The Spartan king tried hard to stop the violation of the maidens under his care – indeed he tried so hard that he was killed in the fracas. The women were raped, and later killed themselves from shame. Under such circumstances one can well imagine the fury and outrage of the Spartans, especially as the Messenians refused to admit their guilt.

The Messenians had a totally different version of events. According to the Messenians the whole thing was a diabolical plot by King Teleclus, inspired by his lust to possess himself of Messenian land. (As we have seen, Teleclus had already a bad reputation in this regard.) Teleclus knew that young Messenians of the highest rank would be celebrating at the temple. This is why he turned up with his maidens. In fact these 'maidens' were young warriors selected by the king because they were young enough to be still beardless. Tricked out in dresses and bangles, these lads each made a beeline for a selected Messenian aristocrat with daggers in their robes and murder in mind. The young warriors were betrayed by their own inexperience, and the Messenians saw through the ruse. A short, sharp melee followed in which the youths and the conniving Spartan king were all slain.

Teleclus had not been acting alone in his plot. The Spartan populace as a whole had been consulted and were aware of what their king was planning. This, said the Messenians, was why the Spartans remained passive in the immediate aftermath of the incident at the temple. The Spartans were well aware of their guilt and could not reasonably demand justice for a failed attempt on their part to commit mass murder. It took a generation for Sparta to modify their memories of the event so that the maidens became real women, and their deaths were 'remembered' as the consequence of an intolerable outrage by the Messenians.

'These', sighs Pausanias, 'are the two different versions. Depending how you feel towards either side, believe whichever you prefer.' (*ibid.*)

The events at the Temple of Artemis Limnatis irreparably soured relations between Dorians and Achaeans, and ruined relations which had in any case been amicable but edgy. Thereafter, all it needed was a further incident to take relations over the brink. According to Pausanias, that incident was a mundane case of cattle theft which rapidly escalated into murder, feud, diplomatic breakdown and war.

By this account, a Messenian called Polychares leased some land for cattle ranching off a Laconian villain called Euaiphnos. As soon as the Messenian cattle were on his land, Euaiphnos rounded up the lot and sold them. While Euaiphnos was regretfully explaining to Polychares that the Messenian cattle had been taken by marauding pirates, one of the herdsmen turned up and explained the true version of events. An indignant Polychares demanded that Euaiphnos hand over the money from the sale, and sent his son to accompany Euaiphnos to his home to make sure he came back with the gold. However, Euaiphnos had no intention of parting with his ill-gotten gains, and as soon as he felt that it was safe to do so, he murdered the son of Polychares and fled with his money to Sparta.

All would have ended peacefully if the Spartans had heeded the furious petitions of Polychares to hand over the murderer. However, Euaiphnos presented himself as the Dorian victim of an unreasonable Achaean and whipped up popular sentiment against his extradition. Doubtless the maidens of Artemis Limnatis were frequently mentioned. While the Spartan authorities prevaricated, Polychares took matters into his own hands. He decided that if the Spartans were sheltering his son's murderer, they were as good as murderers themselves. Accordingly he began to execute any local Spartans or Dorian travellers that he could lay his hands on.

Not unexpectedly this caught the attention of the Spartans, who had heretofore been doing their best to pretend that Polychares did not exist. Ambassadors were sent to the Messenian authorities to demand that Polychares be handed over to the Spartans for trial and execution. The Messenians were ready to comply, provided that Euaiphnos was handed to them for similar treatment. The Spartans would not agree, and the ambassadors returned to Sparta empty-handed.

At this point the Spartans began secretly to prepare for war. In Messenia the debate about what to do with Polychares became so furious that one of the nation's leaders was killed in a heated discussion that became a riot between different factions. The surviving leader, King Antiochus, suggested that Spartans and Messenians put the matter to an independent court in Argos. Ominously, this suggestion received no reply from the Spartans. The Spartans had already secretly decided to go to war.

From the Spartan viewpoint, this was justified. Messenia had always been a Laconian dependency, and would have remained so had Cresphontes not cheated on the lottery which put Messenia under his control. As an independent people the Messenians were undependable, violent and impulsive, as shown by the murder of innocent Spartans by Polychares and the unprovoked rape of Spartan maidens a generation before.

Sparta had previously invaded to restore the dynasty of Cresphontes to the Messenian throne. By their subsequent support of the Achaean peoples the turncoat rulers had shown themselves to be unworthy standard-bearers of the Dorian people. Therefore it now behoved the Dorian Spartans to make good on their original mistake of putting Aepytus on the throne instead of subordinating Messenia to Laconia as should have been done according to historical precedent.

Pausanias tells what happened next:

'A few months later King Antiochus died and was succeeded by his son Euphaeus. The Lacedaemonians meanwhile swore amongst themselves an oath that they would conquer Messenia by force of arms. If the war was drawn-out, neither that fact, nor any setbacks – however disastrous – would stop them. Accordingly they made clandestine preparations, using the greatest concealment possible. Then without renouncing [their official] friendship [with Messenia] and without sending heralds to announce the declaration of war, they launched their invasion with a night attack on [the Messenian border town of] Ampheia.'

Pausanias *Guide to Greece* 4.5.8

Chapter Three

The First Messenian War

Thanks to the vagueness and partiality of our sources, we cannot tell if the run-up to war unfolded as Pausanias describes it. We also cannot tell exactly when all this happened, and how it ties in with other significant developments happening within Sparta at this time. Nevertheless the story of Sparta's conquest of Messenia is not a completely lost cause, because we know firstly, that the war happened, and secondly we know what later Greeks thought happened during the war. For our second point, we have to thank the tireless research of Pausanias who had access to information and sources now lost to us. Despite this, we must bear in mind the caveat that the account of the war which follows is, for all the apparent detail, quite possibly a work of imagination as reliable as the account of the Trojan War in Homer's Iliad. Nevertheless, since the Greeks, and especially the Spartans, imagined that events happened roughly as described below, this influenced later Greek views of the Spartans, and the way that the Spartans saw themselves.

The commencement of the war is given as the second year of the ninth Olympiad. Theoretically, this gives us a very precise date. An Olympiad is a period of four years which begins at the start of a year in which the Olympic Games were held. The first Olympiad was not the first Olympic Games, which were allegedly started by Hercules back in the Heroic Age. Instead the first Olympiad dates to 776 BC, the first year in which records were kept of the winners of each event. Because this was a fixed and stable date, many other events in antiquity were given by their Olympiad and year. For example – 'The first year of the seventh Olympiad [752 BC] was when Romulus began his reign as king of Rome.' (Dionysius of Halicarnassus Roman Antiquities 1.75)

Using this dating method, we get the Messenian Wars kicking off in 743 BC. While there has been a great deal of controversy about this – and most other dates given by the Olympiad dating system – the date of 743 BC is likely to be accurate to within a few decades at least, and this much accuracy is pretty good going for the period when classical history was just getting started and almost everything is both vague and controversial.

Again, there is nothing unlikely in the war starting with the surprise seizure of the town of Ampheia. We do not know where this town was, though we can safely assume that it was somewhere on the western (Messenian) side of the Taygetos Range. The town was chosen because control of that location gave the Spartans a base within Messenia with clear lines of communication back to Sparta. In other words, if the Spartans controlled the town they could be assured of a secure bridgehead once they had crossed the steep passes on their side of the range. Had the Messenians maintained control of this town, they could have used it to block Spartan access to their hinterland.

That Ampheia was of extraordinary strategic importance is shown by the extraordinary steps that the Spartans took to secure the place. Firstly, their unannounced surprise attack would have aroused in the Messenians the same indignation that the Americans felt at the Japanese attack on Pearl Harbor in 1941, and it would have aroused corresponding repugnance in the rest of Greece. The proper protocol for declaring war at this time was for the would-be aggressor to send to the opposing nation a herald who would detail his nation's grievances and demand redress. Only if this last-ditch effort at diplomacy failed would the herald then formally inform his audience that they and his nation were now at war.

Of course, had the Spartans done this, it is highly likely that the immediate response of the Messenians would have been to rush reinforcements to Ampheia. By the time the herald arrived in Spartan territory with news of the Messenian rejection of his ultimatum, Ampheia would already have been warned, the gates secured and the walls manned. Only by a surprise attack could Ampheia be taken, so a surprise attack it was, despite the ill-repute that this gave the Spartan name throughout Greece. There is a tradition that Argos later joined the war in support of Messenia (and, as we shall see, archaeological evidence as well). If the Spartans did take Ampheia as described, then this act of treachery might well have swayed the Argive decision to go to war.

Another indication of the importance of Ampheia is that once they had taken the town, the Spartans were ruthless in ensuring their control of it. There was little resistance – the town was not garrisoned and the gates were open. Since this was a night attack most people were in their beds, and those who were still awake fled to the temples for sanctuary. According to Pausanias the Spartans were not interested in prisoners. There would be no Ampheians to later betray the town by signalling or furtively opening a gate to their fellow Messenians, because the people of the town were all butchered wherever they were found. 'Those who escaped were few', Pausanias bleakly concludes.

After this atrocity, it was safe to say that Messenia and Sparta were at war. Furthermore given Sparta's resolve and Messenia's fury, this was always going to be more than the usual semi-recreational sparring which was endemic between rival Greek cities of this era. This was a fight to the finish.

Messenia now moved to a war footing. There would be no repeat of the Ampheian atrocity, because all those towns within reach of the Spartan forces now hastily fortified themselves and remained in a state of high alert thereafter. Consequently, though the Spartans made repeated attempts to seize other towns, they were repelled with casualties. This was unsurprising to both sides, because siege warfare in early Greece was a primitive business which was rarely successful for the attackers. Few towns could be taken by storm, so the usual method was to sit outside and wait for the defenders to run out of food. As the Trojans had demonstrated before, and the Athenians were to demonstrate later, this could take a very long time.

Meanwhile Euphaeus, the Messenian leader, mustered his army at the 'capital' of Stenyclerus. 'Leader' is a more appropriate term than 'king' in this context, for it is unlikely that Messenia was a single political entity. More probably the towns and cities of the nation existed in a loose confederation which only came completely together against an external existential threat such as that now posed by Sparta. Euphaeus seems to have realized that the Spartans, though fewer, had the edge militarily, so rather than engage the enemy directly, he concentrated on building up and training his army. This must have seemed a sound strategy, since Messenia had more men and resources than Sparta and was thus better placed to win a war of attrition.

It helped that the Spartans were also planning for the long term. They had come to conquer, not to raid, and therefore they were not interested in destroying bridges and farm buildings that they already looked on as their own. Instead they looted cattle and helped themselves to the crops, but otherwise left the land intact. The Messenians had no such inhibitions. The Spartans were not a seafaring nation and were outmatched at sea, so the Messenians took to the water, and vindictively raided and pillaged any undefended sites they could find on the coast of Laconia.

The war became a sporadic affair of hit-and-run attacks and occasional unsuccessful sieges. In short, a stalemate. Three years after the commencement of hostilities the Messenian leader decided that his men were experienced enough to venture a full-scale battle. The report of Pausanias is improbable, and seems to be a confused version of a later event, so if this battle occurred at all it seems that it was a close win for the Spartans. The battle itself was not bloody because the heavy infantry on each side did not engage, and on seeing that his side was getting the worse of the encounter, the Messenian leader withdrew his forces to a fortified position.

Matters came to a head the following year. Euphaeus was still determined to resolve matters with a pitched battle, and the Spartans too were eager to wrap things up. There are hints that Sparta was having problems on the northern flank, where Argos was becoming increasingly forthright in its support of Messenia. Should relationships between Sparta and Argos deteriorate much further, the Spartans might end up fighting a war on two fronts. On the bright side the city of Corinth, always a rival of Argos, had taken the Spartan side in the war simply because the Argives supported Messenia. There were also many Arcadians fighting on the Spartan side for the same reason, so in the climactic battle in Messenia the numbers might have been more or less even on each side.

The battle is said to have been fought at the base of the Taygetos Range. This makes sense if this was an attempt by the

Messenians to re-take Ampheia and so cut off at the well-head the flow of Spartans into their country. Again Pausanias gives us an account of the battle, complete with a summary of the speeches of each leader. He then goes on to spoil things by describing the actual battle as a typical phalanx engagement. This seems highly unlikely since the dating of the war makes it clear that the battle happened at a time when the development of the phalanx lay at least fifty years in the future. (The earliest depictions of a proto-phalanx are on Corinthian vases of 650 BC. The typical hoplite panoply of large round shield and stabbing spear seems to have evolved slightly earlier, but the evidence is still too late for all but adventurous time-travellers to have used them in the First Messenian War.)

It is remotely possible that the phalanx did evolve earlier, the evidence has not survived, and the Spartans were the very first to use this novel form of warfare. It is also possible that the battle described by Pausanias happened at a later date when phalanx warfare had already evolved. It is more probable that the sources which Pausanias used were aware that a major battle had taken place and, lacking details, filled these in from their own experience of later warfare.

The battle was reportedly an epic affair. Momentum passed from one side to the other, with each army making gains until the other side, galvanized by the threat of defeat, made a major effort and in turn gained the upper hand. The turning point came when one of the Messenian commanders was killed. Lacking leadership and direction, that wing of the Messenian army became disorganized and demoralized and thereafter rapidly collapsed. The Spartans were now able to concentrate their full force on that part of the Messenian army led by Euphaeus, who had been doing rather well up until then. Rather than face the combined wings of the enemy Euphaeus decided to retire from the field, which he was easily able to do, since the Spartan troops facing him were in no shape to follow up and the infantry from the other wing had not yet engaged. In any case, the battle had taken up the remainder of the day, and the Spartans had no inclination for a night action against an enemy who was more familiar with the terrain. Once again a battle intended to settle things once and for all had ended inconclusively, though slightly in the Spartans' favour.

Indeed, as later events proved, in order to win this battle all the Spartans had to do was avoid losing. The original strategy of Euphaeus had proven flawed. Messenia had indeed more resources and manpower than Laconia, but had proven less efficient at exploiting them. There are indications that Spartan diplomacy had succeeded in keeping some Messenian coastal cities out of the war, and as the Messenians were fighting in their home territory, it was their land, manpower and crops that suffered while Laconia was largely unscathed. Furthermore, Messenia was a loose confederation and at a disadvantage against the more politically-centralized Laconians who were able to pursue their aims more single-mindedly. As a result of these factors it turned out that in the long run it was Sparta rather than Messenia that had the edge in terms of resources and manpower.

This is not to say that the Spartans were not suffering from the political stress induced by the prolonged war. They were suffering – hugely – and it will be seen that the strains of having the army abroad for years on end helped to change Spartan society forever. Nevertheless, even though the Spartans were hurting, the Messenians were suffering more. If indeed Euphaeus had miscalculated, and it was Messenia that lost the war of attrition, then the battle before Ampheia looks as though it was a final roll of the dice with the Messenians desperate to force a conclusion.

> 'After the battle, the Messenians were in serious trouble. The cost of garrisoning towns against the Spartans had exhausted their funds, and their slaves were deserting in large numbers to the Lacedaemonians. They were also alarmed by an outbreak of disease, which though it resembled a plague, did not develop into a full-scale epidemic.'
>
> Pausanias *Guide to Greece* 4.9.1

Without the resources to maintain the defence of their towns, the Messenians withdrew to a fortress of last resort – the ancient mountain stronghold which Homer in the Iliad calls 'stepped Ithome'. Ithome was built into the side of a mountain of the same name, the principal peak of the mountain range on the west of the Pamisos River. According to Messenian tradition, Zeus, King of the Gods, had been brought up on this mountain, which is called Ithome after the name of one of Zeus' nurses. However, in this moment of crisis it was not religious but tactical considerations that drove the Messenians to make their stand at this fortress. Ithome occupied a highly defensible position, and the Messenians were well aware that their freedom depended on making it even more so.

This is not to say that the Messenians neglected the religious aspect. According to Pausanias they sent a messenger to Delphi to ask the Oracle for advice. The reply was a grim one – Messenia would be saved if a maiden of one of the leading families was sacrificed to the Gods of the Underworld. The Messenians were appalled, since human sacrifice was considered abhorrent at this time, though it was an occasional feature of life in the Heroic Age.

A maiden was chosen by lot from among the eligible candidates. Immediately a problem arose – someone stepped forward with information that the supposed mother of the girl was in fact barren. In order to satisfy her husband's desperation for an heir, the mother had faked a pregnancy and produced as her child a foundling whom she had procured elsewhere. During the confusion and controversy which resulted from this declaration, the daughter's father quietly packed a few essentials and then he and his daughter slipped out of town to defect to the Spartans. At this point a member of one of the top aristocratic houses stepped forward and freely offered his daughter as the sacrifice in place of the escaped maiden. (What the daughter felt about this noble act by her father is nowhere recorded.)

Once the Spartans discovered that a maiden had been sacrificed, they, as a gods-fearing folk, were reluctant to put themselves on the wrong side of divinity. For the next five years, therefore they held back from assaulting Ithome. So says Pausanias and if true, the story would certainly reflect well on the Spartans to the rest of Greece, as the Hellenes placed a great deal of value on honouring the will of the gods. It is however also true that archaeology and an alternative tradition show that at around this time the crisis with Argos finally escalated into open warfare. A Spartan army most certainly attacked the

Argolid at this time, and we know that the Argive town of Asine abetted the Spartans in their invasion. (Though formally Argive, the people of Asine were closer in ethnicity to the Spartans.)

In any case, either because the Spartans were otherwise occupied or because they feared the wrath of Apollo, the Messenians gained a respite. However, further information about the 'maiden sacrifice' came to light over the intervening years. It turned out that the 'maiden' had a lover who claimed not only that the girl had ceased being a maiden a while back, but she was actually now carrying his child. This led to a furious argument between lover, who intended to marry the girl, and the father who regarded the lover's claim about his daughter's pregnancy as a direct affront to his honour. Finally the father became so incensed that he murdered the unfortunate girl and sliced her open before witnesses to demonstrate that there was no child within her.

Of course, killing the girl was self-defeating, since in proving that the maiden was eligible to be sacrificed the father had made her permanently unavailable for the deed itself. Euphaeus attempted redeem the situation by claiming that the killing had actually been the intended sacrifice, but this argument failed to convince the Spartans (and it apparently transpired that the gods were not persuaded either). A squalid domestic murder in no way constituted a proper sacrificial offering, so the Spartans were able to cast their religious doubts aside, and they prepared to once more re-enter the fray.

Yet again our sources treat us to the subsequent battle as if it were a traditional hoplite clash from a later era. And yet again this battle was an evenly-matched affair with the advantage passing from side to side. The Spartans again had the upper hand as night fell, but this time, as he attempted to retrieve the situation, Euphaeus was mortally wounded. The Messenians managed to extricate their leader from the battlefield. The poets produced an epic struggle between Spartan and Messenian heroes for the person of the expiring leader, but that leader later died of his wounds. Command of the Messenian forces passed to the self-sacrificing (well, daughter-sacrificing) Aristodemos whom we last encountered standing triumphantly over the empty womb of his slaughtered child.

The sources give some indication that Aristodemos was not everyone's first choice, and that some protested openly about selecting as leader a man polluted by his daughter's blood. However, Aristodemos was able to produce the most effective of arguments to rebut his opponents. By careful planning and the judicious selection of a picked strike force of troops, Messenia's new commander not only took on the Spartans in battle, but soundly defeated them.

Though outdone militarily, and driven back to their original base at Ampheia, the Spartans were in no wise prepared to give up. They sent a group of young men to the Messenians. These youths were to pretend to be deserters seeking sanctuary with the enemy, but were in fact primed to fling open the gates of Ithome at the earliest opportunity. Aristodemos saw right through that one, and sent the 'deserters' straight back to the Spartans, scornfully claiming that though they constantly invented new atrocities, the Spartans' tricks were old.

Eventually however Aristodemos was worn down by Spartan intrigue and propaganda, and by the hostility of Delphi, for since the non-sacrifice of Aristodemos' daughter, the Oracle had been unrelentingly pro-Spartan. A sceptic might note that Delphi could be influenced by the wider world, and especially a larger conflict between two of the main cities on the island of Euboea which had divided the rest of Greece into two hostile camps. (In the Peloponnese this took the form of Sparta, Arcadia and Corinth supporting one city, and Messenia and Argos supporting the other.)

Tradition says that Aristodemos was so overwhelmed by the hopeless futility of the long war and awareness of his personal guilt that he eventually committed suicide, and did so on the tomb of the daughter he had murdered. A more cynical historian might note that Aristodemos was never popular with certain members of the Messenian aristocracy. It is quite possible that a cabal of leaders of the Messenian confederacy staged the suicide in exchange for a well-placed Spartan bribe plus the promise of favourable treatment later. (We note a tradition which says the Spartans also tried to bribe Messenian leaders in a later war.) Also in this context, one notes that when the Spartans did occupy Messenia after this war, certain coastal cities in the area of Pylos were left untouched and continued to operate independently under their pre-war systems of government.

As with most of this war in which we can only make out – dimly – the main outline of the actual events we perforce must leave the rest to speculation. What we are told is that the Messenians were demoralized by the death of Aristodemos - however this came about – and resistance collapsed. Once again the Spartans surged across the country and the Messenians were penned up in Ithome. This time there was to be no relief. After a single large-scale but half-hearted sortie failed, the Messenians endured five months of siege in their mountain fortress, and then broke.

> 'They left their fertile fields, they fled the towering mountains of Ithome', says the Spartan poet Tyrtaeus (of whom we shall hear more later). Pausanias agrees. 'Any who had contacts with Argos, Sikyon or the Arcadians took refuge there … but most of the common people dispersed to their native towns, there to await their fate.' (Pausanias 4.14.1)

This fate was severe, for the Spartans had endured twenty years of warfare, and were not in a forgiving mood. Ithome itself was flattened so that not one brick remained atop another. Then, with the principal focus of their rage destroyed, the Spartans spread across Messenia and brought the other towns of the region under their control.

The people of Messenia were made helots. That is, they were enslaved, but not sold off to individual masters. Instead the state kept control of the helots and allocated them to the fields of Spartiates who were given land in Messenia. Even in those areas where the Spartans did not simply possess themselves of Messenian land, the people did not get off lightly. For 'Like donkeys exhausted under heavy loads they were constrained by force to bring to their masters half of all the produce from their cornfields.' (Tyrtaeus, quoted in Pausanias 4.14.5)

While it seems quite likely that the people of Messenia were indeed subjugated by the Spartan conquest, it is uncertain whether the system of helotage that the land suffered under in later centuries was imposed fully at this time. Likewise, it is unclear what areas of Messenia were brought under direct Spartan control – as has been seen earlier, it seems some coastal regions were allowed to continue more or less as were the *perioiki* of Laconia itself.

Even the duration of the war is suspect. Twenty years make a convenient sum, and emphasise the difficulty of the war by making it exactly twice as long as the siege of Troy. Nevertheless, we do have some archaeological evidence to back up the date of the war's end. After the Spartans had withdrawn from their raid on Argive lands to concentrate on conquering Ithome, the town of Asine, whose people had been collaborators in that Spartan invasion, were left exposed to the wrath of their countrymen. According to the historical tradition, once the Spartans had gone, the people of Argos gathered their army and flattened the city. The survivors of the Argive attack fled to Sparta.

These refugees from Asine took part in the later attacks on Ithome, and after the war the Spartans allowed them to re-found their town in conquered Messenian territory. Around a century ago, the original town of Asine was discovered by archaeologists working in the Argolid. They concluded that Asine had been an ancient settlement from the Mycenaean era which had survived the Dark Age. The history of the town terminates in a destruction layer which has been dated as not later than 700 BC and probably a decade earlier. (Kelly, T. 'The Argive Destruction of Asine', *Historia,* Sep., 1967, pp. 422-431)

Thus we get a twenty-year war which (according to the ancients) started in 743 BC and which finished (according to modern archaeology) around 710 BC. It is not an exact fit, but given that we are looking at events of twenty-seven centuries ago which are mainly based on oral tradition, the dates are rather satisfactorily close.

After twenty brutal years, the Spartans had conquered Messenia. Now they just had to hang on to it.

Chapter Four

Lycurgus

Ask a Spartan why his state had a set of rules and customs so radically different from the rest of the Hellenes, and the answer – with true Laconian brevity – would probably be 'Lycurgus'. Lycurgus was the law-giver, the man who took an everyday, average Greek city, and through his forethought and wisdom radically reshaped the customs of Sparta to make it the morally pure, warlike and superior state which it became.

Or, by an alternate view, Lycurgus was the ultimate control freak whose laws not only covered the constitution of the state but issues such as where, when and how often a man could have sex with his wife, what clothes their children were allowed to wear, and even the conduct of that child when walking down the street. (Head down, both hands concealed, not looking right or left or speaking to anyone.)

Lycurgus dictated what a person could eat at a meal, whom that person could eat it with, how much wine could be consumed as an accompaniment, and that no torches were permitted to light the way home afterwards. Matters such as the length of one's hair were determined by Lycurgus, who even carefully considered obscure matters such as – for example - the number of strings a musician could have on his instrument. (A harpist proposing to enter a competition was once confronted by an official with a knife who enquired whether he should trim the illegal extra strings from the front or back end.) Lycurgus prescribed how often one should go to the gymnasium, and the exercises appropriate for men and women once there. In short, Lycurgus dictated almost every moment of a Spartan's life, whether waking or sleeping (the latter done on a mattress of prescribed type in a crude house which Lycurgus had dictated could be built with no other tools but axe and saw.)

So who was this Lycurgus? Here, things get somewhat more obscure. The Spartans placed him in their distant past. 'Incidentally, this law code is undoubtedly very ancient. We know this because Lycurgus allegedly lived in the time of the Heraclidae [ie around 1000 BC].' So says the Spartanophilic Xenophon, a soldier and historian who wrote in the fourth century BC. (Xenophon *On Sparta* 10.) This claim of great antiquity for Lycurgus is often repeated. Not only did it make his laws and customs seem established for time immemorial, but for modern historians it certainly adds to the law-giver's reputation for sagacity and foresight.

This is because Lycurgus allegedly passed a series of laws about the currency, describing in detail what coinage was permissible for which transactions and of what metal the coins should be made. Furthermore, according to the Spartans' own traditions, Lycurgus did this several centuries before the first Greek coins appear in the archaeological record, making this a feat of intellectual premonition comparable to alleging that during her reign Queen Victoria laid down detailed protocols for twenty-first century internet usage.

The anachronistic arrangements which Lycurgus allegedly made for the use of coinage in Laconia are also seen in the law-giver's equally detailed rules for hoplite warfare and equipment, again many years before Greece saw its first hoplites. This has caused many modern historians to assume that Lycurgus is as fictional as the tooth fairy; a character invented by the Spartan ruling class as a way of giving their laws extra authority. Whenever those rulers wanted to impose a particular rule on Spartan society, they did it by 'recalling' a rhetra of Lycurgus which was not being properly enforced. (The individual laws of Lycurgus were called 'rhetras'.) Conveniently for these secret legislators, it appears that Lycurgus gave his laws orally, so there was no way of checking whether he had actually proposed a given law or not.

In fact, 'Lycurgus never reduced his laws into text. Indeed not – he explicitly [and very conveniently] gave a rhetra which forbade it.' So Plutarch tells us (Plut. Lyc. 13) when he came to write the *Life of Lycurgus* around the start of the second century AD. Plutarch seems sure that Lycurgus did exist, though the prologue which describes the biographer's frustrations in determining more than this basic fact are worth repeating here.

'Nothing can be said about Lycurgus without someone

else disputing it. There are different accounts about when he was born, where he travelled, how he died and – above all – about what he did as a law-giver and politician. Least of all can anyone agree in what times he actually lived. ... Aristotle the Philosopher agrees that he was contemporary with the founder of the Olympic truce (ie the ninth century BC). Those who go by the king-lists of Sparta ... claim that Lycurgus far predates the first Olympiad. Timaeus hypothesizes that there were two people called Lycurgus in Sparta, who lived at different times, and the achievements of both were ascribed to the greater of the two ... some allege that Lycurgus actually met Homer in person.'

Plutarch *Life of Lycurgus* 1

Some modern historians would like Lycurgus to have existed. ('Lycurgus adds a touch of colour which I would be sorry to lose', remarks W.G. Forrest in his *History of Sparta* p.60). For these historians Lycurgus has to have lived and legislated much later than the Spartan tradition dictates. This later date would make his reforms early, but still relevant to matters such as warfare and the currency which the laws describe. The date which fits best is sometime around 650-700 BC, which makes Lycurgus and his reforms very relevant to our narrative, because this is the date immediately after the First Messenian War.

Everyone agrees that the changes which 'Lycurgus' made were revolutionary, and one of the first things a revolutionary needs is enough public unrest to push through his revolution. We have seen that there exist indications that the long war against Messenia produced social strife in Sparta, and it is to two of these indications that we now turn. Was this unrest the catalyst which made Sparta the state it later became?

The first sign that all was not well is the founding of the colony of Taras (modern Taranto) in southern Italy. This was the only major colony which the Spartans founded. According to Spartan tradition this colony was founded immediately after the First Messenian War. The necessity of keeping Messenia under control and maintaining the siege of Ithome – not to mention a military excursion against Argos – had meant that many Spartan warriors had been forced to remain on campaign for years on end without seeing their wives or homes. It came as something of a shock then, when these warriors did come home and found a healthy proportion of their wives nursing toddlers or even well-grown children.

These children were politely called 'Partheniae' – the virgin-born – and such was Sparta's need for manpower that everyone took care not to ask the whereabouts of certain handsome *perioiki* at the time the children were conceived. Many of these children were old enough to fight as soldiers by the end of the war, but once the war actually ended and the main body of Spartan warriors came home, the Partheniae became an embarrassment. Eventually it was decided that these children should leave the city and settle elsewhere. The traditional date for the founding of Taranto is 706 BC, and this, like the destruction of Asine in 710 BC, is one of the dates which has helped later historians determine when the First Messenian War ended.

Colourful as the story of the Partheniae may be, it should be taken with a pinch of salt. However, the basic fact is probably true – that at this time social tensions in Sparta were so acute that certain sections of the population could not stand the sight of each other and the only solution was for one group to move elsewhere.

There is another indication of strife, and this is to be found in the well-known ('well-known' to Spartan historians, anyway) so-called 'rider' to the Great Rhetra. The Great Rhetra is the exception to Lycurgus' law that his decrees should not be written down, because we have the text of this one, perhaps because Lycurgus did not decree it himself, but obtained it from the Oracle at Delphi. The text reads:

'First build a temple dedicated to Zeus Syllanius and Athena Syllania, Separate the people into 'phylai', and allocate them to 'obai', And set up a Gerousia of thirty including the Archagetai.'

This remarkable item of text needs a moment to explain before we continue. Gods had 'aspects' so for example 'Zeus Soter' was Zeus Saviour, and thus a different facet of the deity to Zeus the Thunderer. What aspect is described by the epithet 'Syllania' is now unknown, but it was certainly customary for Greeks of the Archaic and Classical eras to first appease their gods before embarking on any new enterprise or making radical changes.

'Phylai' are tribes (from which root we get the taxonomic designation 'phylum'), and in Spartan society each Phylum was sub-divided into 'obai' – large family units analogous to centralized clans. This social arrangement of tribes and clans is certainly ancient but it also reflects the situation in other Dorian cities, suggesting that it was not created by the Spartan Rhetra but was common to all Dorian peoples. Therefore one suspects that the Great Rhetra described the existing situation in Sparta as an innovation in order to appear that it – the Rhetra itself – dates back to ancient days. By conflating the creation of the Gerousia (a sort of senate, which we shall examine in more detail later) with the formation of the Dorian tribes, the Rhetra gives the 'Gerousia of thirty' an air of hoary antiquity which is probably unmerited.

This is not to say that there was not some sort of 'Council of Elders' in prehistoric Sparta – anthropology shows that almost all primitive tribal societies have some such body. However while the Gerousia probably originated in this way, it – and its relationship with the 'Archagetai' (Spartan kings) – was indeed probably defined and constitutionalized at about the time of the Great Rhetra. This leads to the question of exactly when the Great Rhetra was handed down by the Oracle at Delphi. Tradition tells us this was at the time of Lycurgus, but as we have seen, the 'time of Lycurgus' is anywhere between 1200 BC and 650 BC, and a time-frame of more than half a millennium is not really useful for our purposes.

A date of around 800 BC is appealing because the Rhetra says that once the basic steps detailed above have been taken to regularize Spartan society,

'Then from time to time there shall be a festival of Apollo [Appollazein]
    Between Babyka and Knakion, (Plutarch *Lyc.* 6, quotes Aristotle saying that the Knakion is a river and Babyka is a bridge. This leads to the question of why the bridge and river are not in the same place, but other than this unhelpful explanation we have no real idea of where these locations were.)

> There [at the festival] shall be the introduction and repealing of measures;
> But the Demos [the people] must have the decision and the power.'

Even 800 BC is a very early date for a popular assembly with decision-making power. However such an arrangement is not incredible, especially if it turns out that the aristocracy – the real power in most Archaic Greek societies – disliked the situation and did their best to change it. This dislike brings us to the 'rider' to the Great Rhetra, which states: 'But should the people speak crookedly the Gerousia and Kings should set this aside.'

While the Great Rhetra is usually attributed to Delphi via Lycurgus, the 'rider' is usually attributed to Delphi via the Kings Theopompus and Polydorus. This gives us a date for the 'rider', putting it at about 700 BC, because we know from other sources that Theopompus was king at the end of the First Messenian War. The Rhetra is generally supposed to have worked by proposed legislation being put before the people who voted 'yea' or 'nay' to the measures. 'Speaking crookedly' therefore may have involved the people wanting amendments or codicils which perverted the original intention of the measure.

For those studying the situation later, two major factors are relevant. Firstly, Sparta had some form of crude democratic institutions functioning around the time of the First Messenian War. Secondly, those in power became so exasperated with the voters that they forced through a measure largely nullifying the voters' power – since it is a fair bet that it was up to the Kings and Gerousia whether the people were 'speaking crookedly' (ie disagreeing with them) or 'speaking straight' by voting through the proposals that the Kings and Gerousia wanted.

Thus the origins of the unique society which Sparta became can be found in the years following the First Messenian War. Firstly, we have social tension which led, in effect, to the exile of a substantial proportion of the population to the colony of Taras, and an oligarchic coup which largely deprived those remaining in Sparta of their decision-making power. We know that in later years the public land of Sparta was divided into lots called *kleroi*, and each lot was sufficient to maintain one warrior and his family. The Spartiates did not farm or otherwise maintain their land, a job which was left to helots who were also allocated by the state. Thus each Spartiate had land which, in theory, generated the same income. This made every Spartan warrior the equal of every other, since that land was assigned to him at birth.

It seems reasonable to date such a massive and radical re-arrangement of land-holding to the end of the First Messenian War, since otherwise there would have been both winners and losers in the rearrangement, and those who lost land would have complained very bitterly. However, if the land needed to ensure that every Spartiate got his share came from the defeated Messenians, then the complaints of the losers would not have mattered anyway.

The acquisition of Messenia catapulted Sparta to the top rank of Greek cities, but this increase in their city's power and influence mattered only to leading Spartans. However, by handing Messenian land to the very warriors who might have to fight to keep it, the Spartan state gave its foot soldiers a very real interest in keeping control of Messenia. As a result the Spartan rank-and-file became obsessive about maintaining the *status quo* which so greatly benefited them. Consequently, an already conservative society became rigidly so, retaining aspects of Archaic Greek culture which the fast-evolving world of Classical Greece elsewhere left behind.

The Spartan Constitution

By this hypothesis, the so-called 'Spartan Constitution' so admired by reactionaries in later ages developed after the First Messenian War, shaped partly by the social stresses of the war and partly by the division of the spoils of victory after it. Sparta's leaders used the legendary person of Lycurgus to legitimise the measures which they took to control unrest, emphasizing some traditions and subordinating or perverting others, all the while describing their quasi-revolution as a 'return' to the traditional values handed down by the legendary law-giver. The description of Spartan government which follows certainly describes the Spartan system of the early fifth century, and the start of the seventh century is as good a time as any to suppose that this is when that constitution took the form it did.

For what it is worth, Aristotle, writing in the mid-fourth century BC, seems to agree:

> 'For, during the wars of the Lacedaemonians, first against the Argives, and ... Messenians, the men were away from home for a long time. The discipline of military service had prepared them to give themselves over to those making the laws and on the return of peace they submitted to this legislation.'
>
> Aristotle *Politics* 2.9

The Kings

The pinnacle of the Spartan system was occupied by the Kings. Sparta had two of these, probably because the city itself was the amalgamation of two different complexes of villages, each of which kept its own leader. The older village complex is today assumed to be that closer to the Eurotas River, and this produced the Agiad dynasty, from the line of King Agis. The other line was the Eurypontid, from King Eurypon. (We note that at some point in the seventh century the Agiads quietly re-organized the records to transfer Lycurgus from the Eurypontid bloodline to their own. Even though Lycurgus was never King, he was closely enough related to the royal family for the Agiads to want that family to be theirs.)

By and large the dual kingship was successful, because the Kings seldom got under each other's feet. Given the warlike nature of Spartan society – indeed, later Sparta was practically a state built for war – it was usual for one King to lead the army on campaign while the other remained at home and handled domestic administration. This division of labour meant that each King had a pretty clear sphere of responsibility. Conflicts and disagreements were nevertheless inevitable, but these mattered less because the Kings were not autocrats. Indeed, one could make a reasonable argument that true power in Sparta rested with the Ephors.

The Ephors

There were five Ephors, who were elected from among the

Spartiates (those who held kleroi and served in the army). The Ephors served for a year and could not be re-elected. Arguably the main job of the Ephors was to serve as a check on the power of the Kings. If the Ephors felt that a King was not properly behaving himself, they had the right to arrest His Majesty and put him on trial for his misdeeds. In many ways the Ephors also served as the Spartan governing council. We are told by ancient writers that when embassies came to the Spartans they presented their case to the Ephors rather than to the Kings. If the Ephors felt that the matter deserved further consideration they would present it to the Gerousia, over which they themselves presided. The better to keep an eye on the King, two Ephors always accompanied him on military campaigns.

The general division of any government is into the legislative, judicial and executive arms. Since from the Spartan viewpoint the Laws had been laid down by Lycurgus and were immutable, no legislation was needed. However, the Ephors would 'interpret' these laws as required. The Ephors dominated the judicial process, not only because they personally took charge of major cases (in which they were sometimes both prosecutors and judges) but because they had the power to arbitrarily punish any Spartan for perceived infractions of the Lycurgan code. The Ephors also constituted the executive branch of government, though they were required to also consult with the Gerousia on occasion.

We are indebted to Aristotle for his thorough and sceptical review of the Spartan system, since many other writers such as Plato, Plutarch and Xenophon are almost slavishly enthusiastic and uncritical about all things Spartan. Aristotle bluntly called the Ephorate a 'defect' of the constitution. Their power, he remarks, is 'excessive and dictatorial'. Since 'anybody can hold the office' declares Aristotle (overlooking the women, helots, *perioiki* and others who made up an estimated eighty-five per cent of those living in Sparta) the judgement of the Ephors was dangerously uncircumscribed by written laws and regulations. The Ephors often avoided the worst rigours of the Spartan lifestyle, which the cynical Aristotle remarks 'are set to so unrealistically high a standard that the other Spartans cannot really live up to it. In secret they get around the law and indulge in sensual enjoyments.' (Aristotle *Politics* 2.9 *passim*)

In the ancient sources, the actions of the Spartan state are generally assumed to be initiatives of the Ephors, unless the decision of a King is explicitly mentioned. The election of the Ephors was by a method which Aristotle dismisses as 'childish' and open to abuse. That is, a panel of judges was secluded from the mass of electors, able to hear but not see the voters. As each candidate for the Ephorate was presented anonymously and in random order to the people, the judges measured the volume of applause for each man. Those getting the loudest cheers counted as elected.

It is uncertain when the office of Ephor was constituted. Some writers (inevitably) date the institution to Lycurgus, while others believe it was later. It is significant that the Great Rhetra makes no mention of the office, and this makes it more credible that the Ephors were a 'democratic' concession in the settlement after the First Messenian War. This fits with the idea suggested by other ancient sources that the Ephors date back to King Theopompus, and the late eighth century. It should be noted that Spartan records place both Theopompus and the first recorded Ephors to around 750 BC, while our hypothesis puts both nearer to 700 BC. In this context it is worth observing that some later Kings (each of whom ruled for a suspiciously neat twenty-five years) were almost certainly inserted into the king-lists to push the date of Theopompus further into the past, and the Ephor lists look equally unreliable for the early years. (Spartan years were dated by the leading Ephor of that year, so a name - even if invented – was still needed for years where actual records were flimsy.)

The Spartans had no truck with civil disobedience or dissent of any kind, and thus the more important and respected a man, the faster he was expected to leap to obey the Ephors, no matter how unreasonable their demands. The root of the word 'Ephor' is a word which means something like 'guardian', so it is no surprise that Plato called the supreme rulers 'Guardians' in his *Republic* – a vision of an 'ideal' state which incorporated some of the most extreme principles of the Spartan system.

The Gerousia

Supposedly created by Lycurgus (naturally), the first mention of the Gerousia in Sparta is in the Great Rhetra. While the Great Rhetra allegedly sets up the institution, it is more probable that it formalized a body already in existence, and perhaps also standardized the number of members at twenty-eight, plus the two kings. In keeping with Spartan notions of democracy, membership was open to any Spartiate, but this time with the additional restriction that candidates had to be over the age of sixty. Election was by acclamation, as with the Ephors, but unlike the Ephors who served for a year, once elected, members of the Gerousia were there for life.

The Gerousia served as the jury in important law cases, including those rare occasions when the Ephors decided to put a King on trial. Another power of the Gerousia, bestowed by the 'rider' to the Great Rhetra, was to consider the decisions of the Spartiates in public assembly and decide whether or not to veto them. It is also probable that it was the Gerousia which decided what measures should be put to the assembly in the first place.

Aristotle shows his usual scepticism, and believed that appointment for life was a bad idea. 'The mind grows old just as does the body, and since these men have been educated in such a manner that even the rulers cannot trust them, they represent a positive danger.' (*ibid*.) We shall turn to Spartan education later, for it is arguable that the Spartan system of raising children did not develop at this time but as a reaction to events after 700 BC.

Summary

When we look at the Spartan political system, it is evident that it was at some point radically re-structured, rather as the Athenian state was reconstructed almost a century later by the laws of Solon. The Spartan political revolution came earlier because the extreme social stress induced by the long and bitter war against Messenia caused enough dissatisfaction with the state for its members to be amenable to a thorough re-organization. This re-organization was made easier by the expulsion of malcontents to the colony at Taras, and by rewarding the remainder with plots of land in the newly conquered territory of Messenia.

The Kings Theopompus and Polydorus are the main suspects for those who accomplished this reformation, though the pair must have worked closely with other leading men in Sparta. Rather than present their reforms as a new development, they took care to present their innovations as a 'return' to the previously neglected diktats of the legendary law-giver Lycurgus. (In roughly the same way, when Augustus set up the imperial system in Rome during the period 32-21 BC, he called his programme 'the restoration of the Republic', and carefully stressed the ancient precedents for each of his measures.) We note however, that both the rider to the Great Rhetra and the institution of the Ephors are attributed by some ancient writers (e.g. Plutarch) to Theopompus and Polydorus.

The state which emerged from the changes of 700 BC was, if anything highly advanced for an Archaic Greek society. True, the Kings remained as a hangover from a more primitive era, but their power was highly constrained, both by the institution of the Ephors and by the existence of a popular assembly. Not many ancient states of this period had anything resembling a democratic forum which could vote on legislation. Therefore the Spartans were certainly innovators in this regard – even though the origin of this innovation was probably that a large number of disgruntled citizen-soldiers who were very good with weapons insisted on being consulted about what their leaders were proposing, and their insistence was very hard to ignore.

Still, there were two nominal leaders in the form of the Kings, and beneath these, and carefully overseeing their actions were the Ephors – who constituted an elected body with a limited time in office. (Another huge innovation well in advance of contemporary political thought.) Along with the Ephors were the Gerousia, another elected body to which one might assume many former Ephors were elected. As a constitution this allowed clearly demarcated and efficient interaction between executive and judiciary, and also equitably divided power between those who controlled it (the leading men in the state) and those who supplied it (the average Spartan warrior).

Another less savoury development, though not an innovation, was the extension of the institution of helotage to take in the conquered Messenian people. It was rare for Greek cities to permanently take over the lands of another city, and even rarer for them to enslave the former owners while ruling the lands through central government. For example, when the Athenians took over another city in later centuries, they did so by ejecting the current inhabitants and installing their own population as a colony. The Spartans did not do this. Instead they left the former population on its land, but reduced to slavery and controlled by terror. Unsurprisingly, the Messenians took a dim view of this development.

However, despite quirks such as helots and the odd combination of pre-Archaic kingship and precociously democratic institutions, Sparta was still an average Greek city in terms of its society and culture. Poetry, dance and music thrived and the arts were respected. As far as we can see – and that is dimly and not very far – the drastic changes that made Spartan society what it later became had not yet come about. The political and social revolutions were not contemporary. It was to take a dramatic event to make the Spartans become really serious about being Spartans. Nothing less than an existential threat would cause the drastic changes required to turn a relatively normal Greek *polis* into a society single-mindedly organized for warfare. That threat became real a generation later when the Messenians rebelled, and in alliance with Argos, invaded Laconia with the intention of doing to the Spartans what had been done to them.

Chapter Five

The Second Messenian War

Throughout history, when two states with very similar peoples and cultures are placed alongside one another, these two states have a tendency to fight each other with a ferocity and enduring hatred which more distant peoples with a different culture are spared. This was certainly true of the Argives and Spartans. Both Argos and Sparta were ancient settlements (Argos was settled sometime in the early Neolithic Age) and both were occupied by Dorian tribesmen during the Dark Ages. Both states had common customs, gods, and styles of warfare. Despite having so much in common – or perhaps because they had so much in common – Spartans and Argives fought like two scorpions in a bottle.

In the early seventh century Argos was in a period of growth. Although not on the coast itself, Argos was served by the harbour settlement of Napalia which was just 11 km (7 miles away.) Thus, unlike Sparta, Argos had wealth from trade to draw upon as well as the agricultural wealth of the fertile Argolid plain, the cities of which Argos was at this time drawing more strongly into its orbit.

As a strong and assertive state, Argos was particularly disturbed by the Spartan conquest of Messenia. With that conquest, a city long considered a lesser neighbour to the south had suddenly become the equal of Argos in power. The Argives were already somewhat resentful of the Spartans for the rough handling they had received for their support of Messenia in the First Messenian War. (It will be recalled that the Spartans had taken time off from besieging Mount Ithome to launch an expeditionary raid into the Argolid.) It is a fair bet that, even two generations later, there were plenty of Argives who were itching to return the favour.

It was natural then, that those disaffected Messenians smarting under the stringent rule of the Spartans should find sympathetic allies in the Argives, and that the two states would consider combining their forces to crush Sparta once and for all. If, for example, Laconia could be successfully invaded and subjugated towns such as Helos freed from Spartan rule, then Sparta would be no longer a Greek city of the first rank, but one of several minor cities struggling for dominance in Laconia and of little interest or danger to the rest of the Peloponnese. Indeed, if this major demotion in status was all that the Messenians had in mind should they win, the Spartans would be getting off lightly – something of which the Spartans were well aware.

Exactly when the Messenians, backed by the Argives, rose in rebellion is unknown. One indication we have is from the verses of the contemporary Spartan poet Tyrtaeus, whose lyrics urging the Spartans to fight became virtual anthems to later generations of Spartiates. According to Tyrtaeus, Messenia was first won 'by the warrior fathers of our fathers' or two generations before his time. However, poets are not historians, and the lines of the poet might have been chosen more for scansion than historical accuracy. Nevertheless, Pausanias – who is more of a historian – agrees with Tyrtaeus, and places the rebellion in the fourth year of the twenty-third Olympiad, or 685 BC (Paus. 4.15.2). Pausanias also shows us his calculations, in which he discusses and eliminates alternative dates for the rebellion.

Modern historians either agree with Pausanias or place the rebellion a generation later, around 660 BC. This later date coincides with the rule in Argos of Pheidon the Tyrant and was the era in which Argos was arguably at its strongest. (A 'tyrant' in the contemporary sense was not an unjust ruler, but one who had seized the kingship by force though not of the royal family.) As will be seen, the Argives beat up the Spartans quite handily at this point, so the question remains open as to whether the defeat of the Spartans by the Argives inspired the Messenians to revolt, or whether the Spartans were defeated later because they were debilitated from suppressing the Messenian revolt.

In this text we shall be following the argument of Pausanias, because he had access to sources now lost to us; he evidently examined those sources carefully and sceptically, and his reasoning seems sound. Therefore he should be believed unless there is explicit evidence to doubt him, which there is not. So –

'In so desperate a situation were the Messenians, who saw

that the Spartans intended to treat them without mercy, that they saw no other solutions than to either flee the Peloponnese altogether or to revolt. They decided to attempt the latter, no matter what it cost them. The main instigators were young men who, having no experience of the horrors of war, were of a bold spirit and felt that the risk of death was worth it for the chance to live in a free country.'

Pausanias 4.14.6

The leader of the Messenians was a young man called Aristomenes (not to be confused with the last king of the Messenians in the previous war who was called Aristodemos). This young man had in fact a better claim to be the Messenian leader than his daughter-slaying predecessor, as Aristomenes was allegedly of the Aepytid line of the former dynasty. (p.21)

It appears that the Messenians planned their revolt carefully. They had ensured that the Argives would ally with them and they also appear to have ensured the support, or at least the neutrality of those coastal cities of the region which were as yet not under Spartan control. One indication that this was a planned rather than a spontaneous uprising is that it appears to have taken the Spartans by surprise, and in consequence it was the better-organized Messenians who won the first victory of the war at a place called Derai. The whereabouts of Derai are unknown, and since the etymology of the place means something like 'the hillock', the lumpy local topography has no shortage of candidates for the battle site. We do not even know for certain whether the battle was fought in Messenia or Laconia.

One thing that we do know from the local topography is that the arrangement of the Taygetos Range makes it much easier to get to Sparta from Messenia than it is to get from Sparta to Messenia. The former journey consists of a slow upward climb followed by a short sharp descent, and it is much easier to force one's way downhill than upward, especially if at the head of a recently victorious army. Therefore, even though we know there was a place called Deres in Laconia, and that Aristomenes dedicated spoils from the battle at a temple within Laconia soon afterwards, we need not assume that the battle of Derai/Deres was fought in Laconia, though the Messenians were certainly in Laconia shortly thereafter.

How things went for the rest of the year is not known, other than one significant development. According to tradition, the Spartans were prompted by Delphi to send to the Athenians for a war leader. The Athenians were somewhat nonplussed, since they had no desire for Greece to reacquire the major power that Sparta plus Messenia equalled, but they were also too well aware of the penalties for refusing Delphi not to send someone. So they settled for a lame poet of elegiac verse called Tyrtaeus, on the basis that he was the worst war leader that they could think of.

Naturally far-seeing Delphi had foreseen that the Athenians would do this. What the Athenians did not know was that the Spartans had no shortage of capable leaders for the actual command. What they lacked was a poet who would inspire and rally the demoralized Spartan army. Which is what Tyrtaeus did. However, if Delphi had asked the Athenians to send a poet, they would probably have sent a general. So the oracle applied a bit of reverse psychology, the Spartans got the person they needed, and the Athenians learned not to mess with Apollo (whose oracle Delphi was).

This story is so far-fetched that most modern historians reject it outright, though the almost universal acceptance of the story by ancient sources (e.g. Diodorus Siculus' *History* 15.66, or our own Pausanias 4.15.3) must give one pause. Fortunately the geographer Strabo comes to our rescue by robustly claiming the entire story to be rubbish, and pointing out examples from Tyrtaeus' own poetry which suggest that he was a native Laconian.

> 'He says that he himself [i.e. Tyrtaeus] was the Lacedaemonian general in the war, and in his elegy called *'Eunomia'* he tells us that he came from there.'
>
> Strabo *Geography* 8.10

This controversy over the origins of Tyrtaeus is significant, not only because it shows again how obscure our sources are for the late Archaic era, but also because it shows how later Greeks thought of Sparta. At the time of the Messenian war elegiac poetry was a very new development – indeed, by most counts Tyrtaeus was only the second poet to master the form. The idea that Sparta and a native Spartan might be at the forefront of an artistic intellectual movement so boggled the minds of later Greeks that they were prepared to believe any alternative story, however ridiculous.

We have little to no information about most military actions in this campaign. The Spartans evidently drove the Messenians out of Laconia, for the next major action we hear of was in the Messenian heartland, near the old capital of Stenyclerus. The Battle of the Boar's Tomb is so named because it took place near a monument dedicated to an eponymous episode in the legend of Hercules, and here again the generalship of Aristomenes brought about a resounding Spartan defeat. (In which case, it appears that the Athenian assessment of Tyrtaeus as a general was pretty sound.)

However Tyrtaeus proved his worth elsewhere, for with the Spartans outnumbered and defeatist sentiment on the rise, he rallied national sentiment with a series of stirring verses.

'Let us then, advance behind our hollow shields like a swarm of locusts
Pamphyli, Hylleis, and Dymanes; each [Dorian] tribe brandishing the man-slaying ashen spears.
And trusting all to the Immortal Gods, we shall evermore obey our divinely ordained leader.
Come the moment when all shall be wielding the flail, standing up to the spearmen
Dire will be clash when each side strikes rounded shield against rounded shield,
See, they fall one upon another, stabbing men's breasts
And none shall retreat from the pounding, the battering of the great stones
which they hurl, for this their helms can withstand.'
(Rough reconstruction from a very battered papyrus of the third century BC.)

After his victory, Aristomenes dedicated his shield at the sanctuary of Delphi, where Pausanias claims to have seen it personally. 'Upon it is an eagle with wings outspread so that they touch the rim.' Aristomenes had lost that shield in the battle, and went to considerable effort to retrieve it. This was because the shield of a heavy infantryman was a bulky object, and the first thing that one discarded when running away. Aristomenes wanted to avoid the implication of cowardice, though contemporaries elsewhere in Greece were less bashful. The contemporary poet Archilochus lost his shield as he fled a lost battle, and he remarked of the fact:

'Some Thracian now has the pleasure of owning the shield, I unwillingly threw into the bushes. It was a perfectly good shield, but I had to save myself. Let it go. Why care about that shield?
    I will get another just as good.'

It says something of the changing mood of the Spartans that such sentiments were now unacceptable. Archilochus was the foremost poet of his day, mentioned in the same breath as Homer. But with Tyrtaeus stressing the importance of holding the battle-line shoulder-to-shoulder with one's comrades, the Spartans had no time for self-declared 'cowards'. When Archilochus visited Sparta, the Ephors ordered him out of town. (Valerius Maximus 6.3) For the first time, but very far from the last, the arts and intelligentsia were deemed a threat to the warlike proclivities of the Spartan nation.

We shall omit various feats of legendary derring-do by Aristomenes over the subsequent year, in which – for example – he was captured by temple maidens, but escaped by burning through his bonds (or alternatively because the chief priestess was in love with him). Not only are these tales highly dubious, but they tell us little about contemporary Sparta, which is the focus of our narrative.

A more memorable event occurred at the next action, which took place at a place called the Great Trench (location unknown, naturally). This battle was a Spartan victory. It would have deeply satisfied Tyrtaeus if the battle had been won by the new Spartan warrior ethos, in which the Spartans bravely overwhelmed the enemy with their discipline and fortitude. Sadly this was not the case. The Spartans won because they bribed a Messenian ally to betray his own side.

By this stage of the war, as often happens, those regional powers interested in the outcome of the war had become involved themselves. The Argives were backing the Messenians, so the Corinthians, purely out of dislike for Argos, had taken the Spartan side. This was enough to cause the Arcadians – who loathed the Corinthians – to support the Messenians.

The Arcadian leader was an aristocrat called, well, Aristocrates. After quiet negotiations with the Spartans before the battle, the newly-enriched Aristocrates let his men take their place in the battle line as planned. Then, as the Spartans advanced, Aristocrates suddenly announced that his troops were placed in an unfavourable position. Furthermore, the omens before the battle presaged disaster, and therefore the Arcadians should fall back immediately. After this pronouncement Aristocrates promptly led his men into retreat, deliberately choosing a route that took his men through the Messenian ranks. This caused chaos all round, and the problem was promptly compounded by the Spartans who had been waiting for exactly this development. They fell upon the confused Messenians, who were never given the chance to pull their disorganized ranks together. The battle quickly became a rout and the Messenians were defeated with heavy casualties.

Pausanias remarks sniffily;

'As far as we know the Spartans were the first to buy a victory through bribing an enemy, and the first to make victory in war a matter of purchase. They committed this crime in the Messenian War with the treachery of Aristocrates the Arcadian. Up until that time, battles had been won through valour and the favour of the gods.'

Pausanias 4.17.2ff

Aristomenes had learned from the experiences of previous generations in the First Messenian War that it was a good idea to have a bolt-hole in case the Spartans came out on top. Ithome having been effectively flattened beyond repair, and in any case having failed the Messenians once before, a new stronghold had been prepared at Mount Eira. This was in the south-western Peloponnese, and had the advantage of good communications with the still largely independent port at Pylos.

Thereafter the Messenians fought a war of attrition, which they could do because the Spartans were stretched. The Spartan army had to hold down most of Messenia, which they had now reconquered. They had also to have a standing army ready in case the Arcadians, or more seriously, the Argives staged an attack, and they had to besiege Mount Eira. Of the three, Mount Eira took the lower priority, so Aristomenes and his men frequently broke out on extended raids in which they devastated Messenian farmlands. These farms were lands upon which the Spartans were now relying to support their extended army, so the predations of Aristomenes caused considerable hardship in Sparta.

Again, we can discount most of the legendary escapades of Aristomenes in this period, but one tale rings true, given the flexible morality of the Spartan leadership at this time. The two sides agreed a month-long ceasefire so that both could celebrate a religious festival. The Spartans scrupulously ensured that none of their forces made any hostile moves during this time. They did however 'discharge' their Cretan mercenary bowmen. These men were therefore not technically part of the Spartan forces when they ambushed and captured the unsuspecting Aristomenes. Fortunately for the Messenian leader he was rescued by sympathizers before the Cretans returned with their captive to 're-enlist' under the Spartan banner.

This tale may or may not be authentic, but there is an underlying truth. While determined to hold citizens of the Spartan state to the highest ethical standards, Sparta's leaders were even more determined that there should continue to be a Spartan state to do that holding. Accordingly, from start to finish in Sparta's history, the Spartan leaders took whatever steps were necessary to win, however appalling those steps might be from an ethical or moral standpoint. (Further examples will follow in due course.)

The fall of Mount Eira happened after yet another epic siege, this time of eleven years. According to Pausanias (our only consistent source for the period), treachery was again the Messenian downfall. This time a Spartan deserter discovered that Messenian guards had abandoned their posts during a heavy rainstorm. Armed with this information, the man promptly re-deserted back to the Spartan side and led the attackers to the weak spot in the defences. Help from Arcadia, which the Messenians had hoped for, did not arrive because the Arcadian leader was still Aristocrates, and he had taken yet another substantial Spartan bribe to keep his people out of the war.

With the fall of their last stronghold, many Messenians fled the Peloponnese rather than submit to Spartan domination. According to legend, many of them ended up in the Greek city of Zancle on the north-east coast of Sicily. Eventually, in memory of their lost homeland, the population changed the name of the city to Messina – as the city is still called today. Aristomenes did not join the exiles, but remained in Southern Greece, attempting to rally resistance against the Spartans until his illness and death.

'When the Lacedaemonians had taken possession of Messenia they divided the whole land among themselves, apart from the land they had already given to the people of Asine. Also they bestowed [the town of] Mothone upon the men of Napalia, for these people had recently been driven into exile by the Argives. The Messenians whom the Spartans captured in the countryside were forced into Helotage.'

Pausanias 4.24.4ff

It had been a hard-fought war, with the outcome often in doubt, but the Spartans had again triumphed. However, there was not a lot to be proud of in the way that the Spartans had triumphed. This may be why the later tradition made much of the poetry of Tyrtaeus and how the Spartans had fought shoulder-to-shoulder like a band of brothers in every battle, while deliberately obscuring how those battles were actually won. History is written by the victors, and in this case the victors had little incentive to preserve the actual chronology and events of their war.

For the same reason we can only mourn the death of surviving contemporary works from Argos, whose history we know almost exclusively from archaeology and outsiders. It appears that, once the Spartans had dealt with the Messenians (and were still bribing the Arcadians out of the war), the Spartans turned the full force of their army on the Argives. By this hypothesis, once they had subdued Messenia, the Spartans headed north. If the plan was to do to Argos as had been done to Messenia, things did not go according to that plan. The two sides met at a place called Hysaia in the Argolid, and the Spartans were so roundly defeated that they made a serious effort to pretend the entire episode never happened.

Indeed, some modern historians remain dubious as to whether the battle was not an invention of Argive propaganda. However, archaeology and ancient reports (Pausanias again) of numerous contemporary Lacedaemonian grave sites suggest otherwise. 'The case for scepticism is ultimately unconvincing', remarks the modern historian Michael Crawford after his examination of the evidence. (P.118 *Archaic and Classical Greece: A Selection of Ancient Sources in Translation*, Michael H. Crawford, David Whitehead, CUP 1983) Though the Argives might have given the Spartans a substantial setback, the Messenian wars had amply demonstrated the Spartan talent for grim perseverance. No-one in Argos doubted that the enemy would return – Argos had not seen its last Spartan invaders.

Alcman

The culture of Sparta was changing, but it was changing slowly. Tyrtaeus in his poetry argued that 'with the clash of steel comes the playing of the lyre' – in other words that the violence of war should be balanced by the pleasures of peace. We have argued that the political reforms of 'Lycurgus' were in place before the outbreak of the Second Messenian War. However, there are several indications that the social diktats of the great reformer had not yet squeezed the creativity out of Spartan life.

One indication which archaeologists have unearthed is in the form of pottery. It is clear that Laconian potters were among the first in Greece – if not the first anywhere – to break with the geometric patterns of Corinthian-style Archaic era pottery and attempt more adventurous designs – designs which are very different from their grimly utilitarian pots of 150 years later. Archaic Spartan creativity also produced some remarkable ivory carvings and distinctive bronzes, both of which forms of art can still be seen today – for example at the Metropolitan Museum of Art in New York. It is possible that these artistic innovations were imported from the kingdom of Lydia in Asia Minor with which the usually introspective Spartans were in the process of establishing close diplomatic and trade relations.

With trade came Alcman, son of Titarus, a slave from Lydia.

Alcman came to Sparta while very young, but it was not long before his genius for poetry became apparent. Freed from slavery by an understanding master, Alcman went on to become the outstanding poet of his day. From his poems we see a different side to life in early Sparta, for Alcman's sensual poems reveal an expert's appreciation of Laconian wines and a fine appreciation of song and dance.

'Oh, you honey-voiced maidens, with your voices so loud and clear,
My limbs can dance me no longer
I wish, so wish, I were a ceryl to fly,
Unflinching in spirit with the kingfishers over the curling wave
The bird of the spring, deep blue as the sea!'

Alcman *frag 26*

(The ceryl was a male kingfisher which, according to legend was carried on the backs of its mates when it was too weak to fly.)

Alcman has an appreciation of women as people, a concept far removed from the brood-mares which later Spartans considered their womenfolk to be. He sees them as playful and tender partners in pleasure and 'At Aphrodite's behest, when the purity of sweet love melts my heart' [Fragment 130] he dedicated verses to their charms. Indeed a later writer remarked, 'he was licentious in things concerning women and in poetry which deals with such things.' (Athenaeus 13.601) Alcman also penned drinking songs such as one to be sung amid 'couches and tables crowned with poppy-cakes, and linseed and sesame, all placed among the golden drinking flagons. ..' [Fragment 138].

In all this was so far from the Sparta known to later ages that it produced a certain cognitive dissonance among readers. The Roman historian Velleius Paterculus bluntly rejected the idea that the banks of the Eurotas could have produced the playful, sensual imagery of these poems.

'Not a single orator of Lacedaemonia was considered to have influence while he lived or was worth remembering after his death. The cities, otherwise so distinguished, were barren of

literary endeavour … and in the case of Alcman, the Spartan
claim to him is false.'

Vell.Pat 1.18.2

And indeed, the Sparta of Alcman was fading, even in his day.
Perceptions were changing. While the Greeks came to see the
Spartans as invincible warriors who effortlessly dominated the
Peloponnese, it seems clear that the Spartans had a very different
view of themselves. The Spartans knew that they were few in
number, and their land none too rich. They owed their primacy
to their domination of Messenia, and there they had a tiger by
the tail.

The subject population of Messenia hated the Spartans, and
would happily pound Sparta to rubble given the slightest
opportunity. Since there were more Messenians than Spartans, the
Messenians had to be kept subdued by the merciless application
of terror. Since this made the Messenians hate the Spartans even
more, more terror was needed to control them in a dysfunctional
downward spiral which eventually forced Sparta to become a
state wholly dedicated to the subjugation to Messenia through
dominance in war. There was little room left for anything else.

As well as Messenia – as though that was not enough – there
was also Argos, rich, populous and threatening, and beyond that
Corinth and rough, unconquerable Arcadia. In short, tiny Sparta
was alone in a dangerous world which both envied Spartan
success and feared Spartan military prowess. The only way that
Sparta could survive, let alone thrive, would be for the Spartans
to become very, very good at being Spartans.

Chapter Six

The Making of a Spartan Warrior

Spartan warriors were made, not born. It is uncertain at what point the famous (or infamous, depending on your point of view) Spartan *agoge* became a system for raising children, but the best guess is some time towards the end of the Second Messenian War. At this time Sparta had become serious about raising children from birth to become warriors, and it was also at this time that the fathers were largely absent, leaving the state to deal with the upbringing of the next generation. In this section we follow a Spartan boy from birth to his accession to the ranks of the *homoioi*, 'the equals' (as all adult Spartan males counted one another).

A lot of what follows is more speculative than many writers on the topic would like their readers to believe. The Spartans were convinced that their system of raising their young was a major factor contributing to the state's military supremacy over the rest of Greece, so they were not at all keen on sharing with the rest of Greece what that system was. Therefore we have no accounts of the Spartan educational system from the people who actually went through it themselves. Instead we have to rely on interested outsiders – mainly Plato, Xenophon, Aristotle and Plutarch.

Of this group, Plutarch has written the most extensively. He is also the furthest out of date, writing half a millennium after the Spartan educational system was first imposed, and apparently unaware that despite Spartan protestations that the Laws of Lycurgus were inviolate and unchanging, the reality was constantly evolving. (Or devolving – it appears that Sparta became a sort of extreme parody of itself in the early Roman Empire.) Consequently much that Plutarch reports as belonging to a timeless, static institution might well have actually developed within his own lifetime.

Plato idealized the Spartan system, and edited his account of that system to match the ideas laid out in his treatise *The*

Republic. The more humanistic Aristotle disagrees vehemently with Plato and spends much of the early part of Book II of the *Politics* ripping into Plato's ideas – and thus indirectly into the Spartan system from which those ideas were derived. (Aristotle reckoned a Spartan-style educational system produced 'brave little beast-like creatures'. Pol. 1338b)

Xenophon appears to be our best bet then, especially when he is backed up by Plutarch. Xenophon saw the contemporary Spartan system in action, and while very biased in the Spartans' favour, he was at least a keen observer. The problem is that, having gone over to the Spartan side, Xenophon might have deliberately made Spartan education seem more unpleasant than it was so as to deter other Greeks from putting something similar into place.

Therefore given our unreliable, biased or anachronistic sources and the total silence of the Spartans themselves, this account of a Spartan upbringing has to be somewhat hypothetical.

In fact we will start well before the boy's birth, with the boy's mother. 'We Spartan women rule our men, because we are the only women who give birth to [real] men.' Thus Gorgo, wife of the Spartan king Leonidas, once informed a visitor. Indeed, given the misogynistic nature of most Greek societies at this time, Spartan women had, if not an easy time of it, at least a very different experience.

> 'Take a young girl who is properly reared in a decent family, who will one day become a mother. In all the rest of the world she is fed on the plainest food obtainable, with minimal additions of meat or flavourings. The girls are taught to either abstain from wine altogether, or at least drink it highly diluted with water.'
>
> Xenophon, *On Sparta.*

Not so in Sparta, where Xenophon assures us that the Spartans believed that 'the primary function of a free-born woman is the production of children.' ((ibid) Therefore:

> 'Lycurgus gave even women as much attention as possible. Unmarried girls were made to exercise by running, wrestling, casting the discus, and hurling the javelin. This

was so that they might have vigorous bodies and wombs in which children could take root and come better to term, and when the time for birth was due, the women might more successfully cope with the travails of child-bearing. In short, he freed them from all softness, delicacy and femininity.'

Plutarch Lycurgus 14

In the rest of Greece, a well-raised girl was practically a walking tent of veiled modesty, so visitors to Sparta were generally appalled by the sight of young women clad in simple knee-length tunics (which gave them the nickname of 'thigh-flashers'). Often this tunic was the single garment each girl possessed, so the girls simply shed them whenever the tunics might get damaged or hinder whatever exercise was currently being undertaken. While this probably caused our hypothetical visitor to swoon, we have the assurance of Plutarch that:

'There was nothing disgraceful about these under-dressed maidens. They were clothed in their modesty, and wanton behaviour was unknown. Indeed the opposite was true, for it gave the girls the habit of simplicity and an earnest desire for a healthy and beautiful body.'

(Ibid)

In part this was because the aforesaid bodies were exhibited at festivals in parades and processions 'while not wearing much'. These were events which the young men attended by necessity – 'the sort of necessity which lovers know', explains Plutarch in his endeavour to make matters bountifully clear.

In due course, naturally, love (or at least lust) led to marriage, though to the rest of the Greeks the Spartan version was typically bizarre. It was also remarkably informal, since marriage in Sparta appears to have dispensed with the dowries common elsewhere in the Greek world. Likewise, marriage lacked much of a formal religious framework. The main criterion was that both bride and groom be healthy, fit, and of good breeding stock. Given that boys and girls would have met during the various events and festivals of Spartan life, as well as during the course of an everyday education (Spartan girls received a state-sponsored education, just as did the boys), those in a prospective marriage pool would have been reasonably well-known to each other.

By some accounts it was the state that decided who would marry whom, others suggest the parents, and a few believe the happy couple had a say in the matter. In any case, the girl in question had at least the good fortune to be between the ages of eighteen and twenty, whereas other Greeks felt that having just got through puberty made a girl quite old enough.

However, in choosing a later date for marriage, the Spartans here gave an early demonstration of that talent for empirical scientific observation which was to mark Greek intellectual thought in later centuries. They noted that girls in their late teens and early twenties tended to produce stronger babies than those in early adolescence, and furthermore the mothers had a greater tendency to survive and repeat the experience. Therefore a Spartan woman would usually marry a man in his mid-twenties, around five years her senior, while in the rest of the Greek world a thirty-five year old man might easily end up with a fourteen-year-old bride.

It is likely – given the nature of his upbringing, to which we will come shortly – that the groom's previous sexual experience had been with other males. Therefore on her wedding night an effort was made to put the lad at ease by butching up the bride. The girl's hair was cut boy-style, and she was clad in the rough cloak worn by a Spartan male. (How exactly this was meant to relax the female part of the relationship remains a mystery.)

Then in the dark of the night, the husband would take the girl ('by force' says Plutarch, not explaining how this worked if the girl was willing). The groom would not actually 'take' his bride anywhere, because he was still constrained to live with his fellow warriors in barracks and so had to sneak away for his nocturnal bouts of passion. In theory, a groom could conceive several children before he ever met his wife in daylight (which he was allowed to do once he had reached the age of thirty). Because the authorities ostensibly banned these nocturnal meetings between husband and wife, the pair had constantly to contrive opportunities to break the rules in order to be together.

According to ancient writers, this was a marvellous idea for keeping passion fresh by giving the marriage an illicit feel. More practically, it taught Spartans that their state contained a solid streak of hypocrisy, and the key to breaking rules was not to get caught. As we have seen, Herodotus suspected that this attitude extended to other aspects of the famously frugal and constrained Spartan lifestyle.

In due course, a child would be born since this, rather than to meet the physical and emotional needs of either parent, was the point of the pair getting married to start with. There was also a chance that the child might not be that of the mother's husband. If for any reason the husband was not up to the job of child-production, the wife could and did seek assistance elsewhere. Indeed sometimes the husband would assist in the task of finding a congenial surrogate, though the state insisted that he choose someone of suitable eugenic quality.

> 'Considering how jealously older husbands tend to watch over young wives, he [Lycurgus, naturally] decreed that Spartan custom should be the opposite. It was the job of a non-performing husband to find someone of admirable physical and moral quality to stand in for him and produce children in his stead.
>
> On the other hand, a husband might not particularly desire his wife, but still might want children worthy of his name. Again, the Lawgiver was there for him. He might select another woman – someone else's wife – who was well-born and had healthy offspring, and with the husband's approval and consent, produce his children through her.'
>
> Xenophon *On Sparta*

Actually, the consent of the husband was not always sought. Spartan society seems to have had a relaxed view of adultery, and if this adultery produced a healthy boy, it was counted as a win all round. After all, Helen of Troy, ancient Greece's most famous adulteress, was returned to her home in Sparta at the end of the Trojan war, resumed her wifely role without sanction, and went on to become revered as a local demi-goddess.

Childbirth and infancy in the ancient world was by far the most dangerous time of life. For a Spartan the usual perils were compounded by the hostile scrutiny the child was given soon after birth. The Spartan state had no room for passengers, and a crippled or sickly child might as well not have been born at all. Once the child was born, he was bathed in wine – according to Plutarch this strengthened a healthy child, but was too much for a weakling. Assuming that the new-born survived the experience, he was presented to those members of the Gerousia who were of the child's tribe. If the Gerousia were in doubt of the child's constitution, the mother would be instructed to leave the baby exposed on Mount Taygetus for a while. (Estimates of how long vary from overnight to several days.) If the babe survived this test, he – or she, since the Spartans would have had no interest in defective mothers-to-be – was considered suitable for rearing as a Spartan.

Early childhood appears to have been more of less what any Greek child would have experienced, except that, since the Spartans considered all forms of labour suitable only for slaves and helots, the parents would have had plenty of time to concentrate on child-rearing. (This was indeed different to other Greek states, where children often saw more of slaves and servants than of their parents who were often busy with their own occupations.)

At age seven, all this changed – for the boys, anyway. At this point the child was removed from parental custody and became more or less a ward of the state. Now in the *paides* stage of the *agoge* child-rearing system, it was time for the boy to learn the values of discipline, teamwork, and endurance. There was a certain stress on the latter. The boys were issued with a single cloak as an all-purpose, all-season garment, and slept on rushes they had personally pulled from the river. Their 'family' was a group of boys in the same situation. This group was called a 'herd' (*agelai*) and supervised by a 'herd-master'. Older boys were encouraged to take an interest in the development and discipline of the youngsters, and any bullying, intimidation and general abuse that such a relationship involved was seen as helping to develop the boy's character. Also by way of being helpful, the girls who shared exercises and lessons with the boys were encouraged to publicly mock and pour scorn on anyone they felt to be sub-standard.

The rearing of the boys was regarded to be the task of the entire citizen body. The boys were required to call every adult male 'father'. Aristotle acerbically remarks, 'So every boy had a thousand fathers, he was the responsibility of everyone, and neglected by all.' In fact, every Spartiate had the right to 'remonstrate' with a boy he felt was doing wrong or poorly. The boy had then to report this to his biological father who would usually double the punishment because the boy had let the family down.

As well as regular beatings, the boys were trained to endure hunger. Each group of boys was responsible for gathering their own food for their common table, and since the state deliberately did not provide enough food –

> 'Because they had been trained as boys, in later life they would be able to keep going on an empty stomach if the occasion demanded, and if ordered to live on lean rations they would be able to do so without any dramatic changes in their diet. Rather than demand delicacies, they would readily consume anything put before them, so in the long run, the system was actually healthy.
>
> He [Lycurgus] thought this would shape the boys into fine men of good stature, since this diet created supple limbs rather than a body made tubby by good food. On the other hand, not wanting the boys to actually starve, he allowed them, not to help themselves to what they wanted, but to endeavour to steal it.'
>
> Xenophon *On Sparta.*

Naturally, getting caught while thieving food led to further punishment, and the apocryphal story of the Spartan boy who stole a fox cub. Meeting an adult, this boy allegedly concealed the cub under his cloak, and carried on a conversation with the man while stoically concealing the fact that the cub was gnawing its way into his intestines. The lad expired, but was regarded as a splendid example to future generations.

It is uncertain how much a Spartan education involved reading, writing and arithmetic. However, we know that Spartans would write home on occasion. Also if the average Spartan were barely literate – as some early modern scholars seem to have believed – there is little doubt that other Greeks would have scornfully pointed this out. In fact, since ancient writers concentrated almost exclusively on the differences between the Spartan *agoge* and their own systems, it is fair to assume that anything that was not pointed out was standard educational practice throughout Greece. Nor were Spartans totally uncultured. Outside observers frequently noted the skill of Spartans, both male and female in the chorus and the dance – exercises requiring teamwork in the first case and physical ability in the second.

Recently there has been some push-back among academics who query whether Spartan education could have been as awful as it was alleged to be without producing generations of stunted psychopaths of little use to themselves or the state. It is suggested, for example, that the food-stealing phase was limited to a few weeks of 'survival training' and that parents could take charge of their offspring during the many state holidays and take the boys to the family *kleros* to decompress.

On the other hand we have this gruesome description of Pausanias, who confirms the idea that Spartan boys were given a puppy to raise – and then kill.

> 'Among the Laws of Lycurgus are those laid down in the constitution regulating combat among the youths...
>
> Before they fight, the boys sacrifice in the Phoebaeum ... Here each group of youths sacrifices a puppy to Enyalius [a war God], since they believe that the bravest of domestic beasts is the most acceptable sacrifice to the most valiant of the gods.
>
> At this ceremony the boys also pit trained fighting boars against each other ... Just before noon the next day, they enter the place I have mentioned by crossing bridges. They cast lots the night before to select which bridge each group is to use. In the fight they use their hands, kick, bite, and gouge out the eyes of their opponents. The individual fights are as I have described, but in the general combat they charge violently in order to thrust the others into the water.'
>
> Pausanias *Guide to Greece* 3.14.8

Again, this description by Pausanias was written during Roman imperial times, and may have little relevance to the situation in late Archaic Greece over 500 years before, but it confirms the basic principles of a Spartan education. That is, peer pressure, bullying and mockery were used to enforce strict obedience to defined norms, and individualism was strongly discouraged. At the same time, boys were encouraged to use their initiative for the common good, and to disregard the rules whenever they thought they could get away with it. Bravery and endurance were valued much more highly than intellectual or artistic accomplishment, as demonstrated by the precipitous fall in the quality of items such as poetry and pottery once the *agoge* had tightened its grip on the Spartan consciousness.

At age twelve the budding warrior was further traumatized by being handed over to an older youth with whom he was expected to form a pederastic relationship. While the Greek word *paiderastia* means something like 'the love of boys', Xenophon argues that: 'In Lacedaemon the relationship of lover and beloved resembles that of parent and child, or brotherly love, being totally without a carnal element.' However, Xenophon accepts the rest of Greece will accept that statement with sceptical incredulity: 'Of course, it does not surprise me that some people will just not believe this.'

This older boy was expected to introduce the younger into the ways of adult life, and show how a Spartan warrior was expected to behave. Indeed, at this point the young man was inducted into the army reserve, and therefore formally became a part of Sparta's armed forces. If the lad showed exceptional promise, he might also now take part in the activities of the infamous Spartan *Krypteia*.

Essentially the *Krypteia* – the 'secret ones' – were scouts. Their job was to spy out the enemy and strike to weaken the foe if they saw a chance. They were also agents of terror against the Messenian helot population. The reason for this was that the Ephors every year declared war on Messenia even after Messenia had become a conquered state completely under Spartan control. Thus, when they went secretly on patrol in Messenia, the *Krypteia* were technically working in enemy territory and operated under the rules of war rather than those of civil society.

Therefore (in the Spartans' opinion) the members of the *Krypteia* were justified in killing any helots they caught moving about at night. Also, in order to weaken the 'enemy', it was perfectly legitimate for them to discover whom the other helots looked up to and for them then to kill that man – not because he had broken any laws, but simply because he was respected or successful, and therefore a potential leader of any rebellion. This is one reason why members of the *Krypteia* operated in secret – one need not doubt that they and their families would be prime targets for retaliation if any helot revolt were to take place – and the dread of a helot uprising was never far from the Spartans' consciousness. It was generally believed that those who later became leaders of the Spartan state were mostly drawn from the ranks of those who had served in the *Krypteia* and had personal experience of their nefarious activities.

By now our Spartan youth was fully proficient in the art of warfare. He would have been trained how to use the wide, circular shield (*aspis*) which was now becoming the standard equipment of a Greek warrior in the battle-line. This shield was large enough to protect not only the hoplite wielding it, but also partly to give cover to the person standing on the left (which is why lesser armies showed a tendency to shrink from the right-hand side when facing the Spartans). We will examine this panoply in detail later, but for the present it is enough to note that the bulky (30lb / 13kg) shield and long hoplite spear (8ft / 2.5m) were tricky to manoeuvre in close-packed groups such as a battle line.

This was not a problem for most Greek states, since battle mostly consisted of lining up and then hacking away at the opposing line until one side or the other broke and ran. However, the Spartans actually knew and practised drill. They, and they alone, were capable of wheeling from a column to a line, counter-marching and wheeling. (This latter manoeuvre was particularly useful as the Spartans generally crushed the opponents in front of them and then, without losing their own formation, had to turn upon the now-exposed flank of the enemy army facing their allies.) This is where the endless drill and insistence on conformity came into play. The Spartan was accustomed to thinking of himself as part of a unit, and automatically integrated with his fellow warriors so that his group acted as one completely co-ordinated unit. This in itself was something which terrified the Greeks of other cities who were all individualists to a man.

Finally, the Spartan youth moved into the ranks of the *Hebontes*, those young men on the verge of full acceptance into Spartan society. At this point he was expected to take over the running of the *kleros* assigned to him at birth. The production of the *kleros* was an important factor in the new Spartiate's application to join a *syssitia*, one of the communal messes which would thereafter form the core of the Spartiate's social life. The mess was more than a place where a Spartan ate together with his fellow warriors. It also formed a military unit in the Spartan army, and until he was accepted into a *syssitia* a Spartan did not count as a fully-fledged citizen. When a member of the mess, the Spartiate was expected to contribute to the running costs by contributions of food and other materials from his *kleros*, so a well-run farm was as important as good backers and high social standing when the youth applied to the mess of his choice.

Once accepted, the young man was in a position to seek a wife and the cycle would repeat itself once more.

The Spartan *agoge* has been controversial almost from the time it was first implemented until the present day. Even now there exist embittered survivors of certain British boarding schools whose founders believed that the basic principles of the Spartan educational system were the ideal way to produce upstanding leaders for the next generation.

The Spartan system was undoubtedly successful in its intention of producing the finest warriors anywhere in the known world. While the personal cost to some individuals may have been high, for every boy who suffered under the system there would have been others who rose to the occasion, gloried in the challenges and rather enjoyed the whole thing. After all, while the training of modern elite military units takes place among older individuals, no-one suggests that this training should do anything but demand the uttermost from the physical and mental resources of the participants. Yet these units have no shortage of volunteers. Perhaps Spartan boys also felt that the privations they suffered were worth it to join the ranks of the most respected and feared people in Greece.

Furthermore, whatever its deficiencies in kindness, the Spartans created what was quite possibly the world's first state-sponsored educational system. Unlike the situation in the rest of Greece, a child's educational progress depended more on his own abilities than upon the resources of his parents. If one Spartan was better-educated than another, it was because he had better made use of the same resources that were available to all. The fact that 'all' included girls was another innovation which, even if done only for the most pragmatic of reasons, nevertheless makes Spartan society outstanding in a culture which regarded women with condescension bordering on disdain.

Furthermore, the Spartan system aimed not at producing mindless automata for a totalitarian regime, but independent individuals capable of demonstrating initiative and expressing their own opinions when the situation required it. While obedience was seen as an outstanding virtue on a par with self-sacrifice, the Spartans were also taught that no man was their superior by nature. Rather their state fully took on board the maxim 'If you would command, first learn to obey'. A Spartan fully complied with the orders of the Ephors and the Gerousia, but the Ephors did not hold office for long, and a Spartan might have hopes of joining the Gerousia himself one day. Meanwhile, his voice in the assembly counted for as much as the next man's.

The only Spartans who could count themselves as better than anyone else were the Kings, the successors of the Agiad and Eurypontid lines. Significantly, the Kings were the only Spartans who were not forced to endure the *agoge* system of education.

Chapter Seven

Domination of the Peloponnese

Arcadia

Messenia did not take up the whole of the south-western Peloponnese – this fact is evident from the etymology of the name alone, which must be something like 'Mid-land'. Therefore the Spartan conquest of Messenia did not mean that the entire southern Peloponnese was now in Spartan hands, but merely that the major obstacle to Spartan absorption of the rest had now been removed. Therefore it is probable that the years following the Second Messenian War were spent in the slow city-by-city conquest of the independent towns such as Pylos and Mothone and tribes west of the Selas River. How each of these peoples came to terms with the Spartans would have determined whether they were fated to become *perioiki* – subject to Sparta but nominally independent within their own municipality – or helots owned along with their lands by the Spartan state.

Exactly what happened here is totally missing from the pages of history, since the matter was of little interest to those Greeks elsewhere, and the Spartans were disinclined to tell others what they were up to. However, it is clear that by around 630 BC at the latest, all of the Peloponnese south of Arcadia could be counted as Lacedaemonia, a single political entity that consisted of Sparta, Laconia, Messenia, and lands to the west. In turn the peoples of Lacedaemonia consisted of Spartiates, Perioiki, helots and slaves. (The difference between the latter two categories was mostly that the helots were legally bound to their land, and the slaves were legally bound to their masters.)

If the hypothesis is correct that this was the point when the *agoge* was firmly bedded into Spartan society as a stratified form of warrior training, this would be partly explained by the fact that much of Sparta's manpower was away. Thus the next generation had to be trained by the state, as the children's fathers were elsewhere, wrapping up the conquest of the south-western

Peloponnese, and holding down the lands which Sparta already occupied.

The difficulty of the latter task can be summarized by the standard Spartan rule that every Spartiate should be able to defeat eight helots. The best we can do with demographics from the period is to make a rough guess that the helot population of Messenia and Laconia outnumbered the Spartans by about five to one. However the Spartans would not be able to focus their entire power on the helots should they rise again – now that Sparta was a major power in Greece it was almost certain that as soon as Sparta got into difficulties, jealous or insecure neighbours would immediately pile in against Sparta. The rest of the army would be needed to fight them off.

The Spartan view was that theirs was a small *polis* surrounded by enemies both internal and external. The Spartans only held on to their ascendency through sheer willpower and military ability. This attitude was formed early and ran deep. It was expressly stated by a general called Brasidas during the later war with Athens. Brasidas informed his men:

'You are expected to be brave in war, because it is your birthright. Where you come from, it is not the few who are ruled by the majority but exactly the other way around. Battle and conquest, and only these things, are the foundation of what makes our nation powerful.' (Thuc. 4.126)

Given this warrior ethos, and the fact that the only way that a state can properly prepare for war is by actually doing some fighting, it is unsurprising that, once the southern Peloponnese was securely under their state's control, the Spartans looked around for a further target for their aggression. There are some indications that the Spartans interfered in a war between the Eleans and Pisatans around 570 BC. These two peoples were struggling for control of Olympia, and the prestigious Olympic Games which were held at that site. It appears that the Spartan intervention tipped the scales and their preferred side – the Elean – was victorious. Sparta had little interest in who held Olympia, but the Pisatans were located close to the northern border of Messenia and had supported refugees and the helot population remaining in Messenia. Therefore the Spartans were happy to slap down what they saw as enemy sympathizers.

In previous generations the Spartans had flexed their expansionist muscle elsewhere in Arcadia, but with mixed results. In the time of Lycurgus (whenever that was) the Spartans were reputed to have taken the town of Aegys. They also captured the mountain town of Phigalia by treachery, but were driven out by a temporary coalition of indignant Arcadians. Furthermore, the Arcadians seem to have compromised the main population of the border towns between the Argolid and Sparta. Given Sparta's previous and largely unsuccessful expansionist efforts in their direction, it is unsurprising that the Arcadians were suspicious and hostile to the Spartans. The Arcadians became even more so once Sparta's corruption of their leader Aristocrates in the Messenian war had been discovered (to the fatal discomfiture of said leader).

Not only the Pisatans but the Arcadians in general were sheltering a large number of dispossessed Messenians who had intermarried into the families of their hosts, uniting the two nations in a common bond of anti-Spartan hostility. From the Spartan viewpoint it was bad enough that they had a hostile Argos to the north-east and a viciously sullen Messenia to the west. The last thing they wanted was a further threat from Arcadia in the north-west.

The long-term Spartan strategic goal at this point may well have been the complete subjugation of the entire Peloponnese. After all, the conquest of Messenia had taken a long time, but it had been worth the effort to gain possession of the fertile lands along the Pamisos River. Indeed, when someone asked Anaxandrias – King of Sparta circa 560–520 BC – why his people left the care of their fields to slaves while they concentrated on warfare, the king asked in reply; 'How do you think we got those fields in the first place?' (Plut. *Saying of the Spartans* Anax. 3).

So the question was, would the approach that had gained Sparta control of Laconia and Messenia work also with the mountains of Arcadia or the cities of the Argolid? And in the conquest of the Argolid, there was also the matter of Argos, the main city of that region. Argos had interfered persistently against Sparta's interests during the Messenian wars, and after the Messenians had been dealt with, the Argives had then had the temerity to beat the Lacedaemonian army at Hysia.

Furthermore, the Argives, like the Spartans themselves, felt that their state was the natural leader of the Peloponnese and that rivals needed putting down firmly and permanently. Therefore if Sparta did not do something about Argos, it was only a matter of time before the Argives marched south to eliminate Sparta. So Argos was certainly on Sparta's 'to do' list. On the other hand, Argos was more than capable of defending itself, and indeed a tentative expedition against the city had recently been given short shrift by Meltas, grandson of the tyrant Pheidon (and the last king of Argos before that city's political reconstruction). Argos would not be easy.

Tegea

Therefore, given Sparta's presumed long-term intentions, the matter became one of priorities. Which should be tackled first in what would in either case be a difficult and drawn-out undertaking – Arcadia or the Argolid? It was a knotty question, so, as did most Greeks of the day when faced with this sort of conundrum, the Spartans asked the Oracle at Delphi for advice. Delphi came back with what appeared to be one of the Oracle's less ambiguous declarations.

'You ask for Arcadia? That's too bold, and granted not to you.
The hardy Arcadians, eaters of acorns, are many –
They'll keep you out.
But I am not grudging, you shall have Tegea
To beat with your feet in rhythm
And her fair plains for your measuring-rope.'

(Herodotus *History* 1.66)

Tegea? This city had certainly interested Sparta's generals before. There are not many approaches to the Eurotas plain of central Laconia, and perhaps the easiest was the road connecting Laconia with Argos. Across that road, and right on the border, sat the city of Tegea. At the intersection of the boundaries between Laconia, Messenia and the Argolid, Tegea dominated the cold, high plain of Tripolitza and the approaches to Lacedaemon from the north.

An ancient city with former pretensions to greatness of its own during the Heroic Age, Tegea was constantly engaged in feuds with the neighbour with which it shared the plain – the city of Mantinea. Indeed, some archaeologists have postulated from the growth pattern of Mantinea that this city had developed rather as had Sparta itself – from a group of villages which combined through necessity. In the Mantinean case, the necessity was to resist encroachments from Tegea.

Thus to the Spartans it seemed that the Oracle had demonstrated fine strategic vision. Whether the Spartans wanted to take over Arcadia or the Argolid, Tegea was a reasonable first step. Not only was Tegea a minor power in its own right, and one sympathetic to the Messenian cause, but once the city was secured, the Spartans would have gained control of what was simultaneously the key access to Laconia and a bridgehead for further expansion. At the same time they would have disposed of a minor but significant threat to their own interests.

Therefore the Spartans marched against Tegea, confident both in the prowess of their army and the backing of the gods. They took with them their measuring ropes, so as to divide the fields of Tegea into *kleroi* for future generations of Spartiates, and fetters with which to secure the prisoners who would work those fields. In making these plans, the usually devout Spartans had overlooked one significant deity – Nemesis, the Goddess who punishes the presumption of pride. The Spartans were not yet anywhere near as good at warfare as they believed that they had become, and they treated their coming victory as a formality. The Tegeans, on the other hand, had the example of Messenia before them and were well aware that their land and their liberty were at stake. They fought like wildcats, and handily defeated the surprised Spartans.

Still, at least the Spartans could console themselves that the Oracle had not lied. Wearing the chains they themselves had brought to Tegea, the Spartan prisoners of war did indeed tramp across the fields they had intended to divide as the spoils of war - but as slave labourers under Tegean overseers. The Spartans did eventually get the prisoners back, but the Tegeans kept the chains. These they hung in their temple of Athena Alea, where Herodotus saw them for himself several generations later. As for their plans for subjugating the entire Peloponnese, the Spartans had just been handed a severe reality check. Even one relatively small city was proving too tough a nut to crack, let alone the rest of the peninsula. Nevertheless, with their usual doggedness the Spartans kept trying. They kept failing too, and finally turned once more to Delphi for help.

This time the Oracle was unambiguously ambiguous, and the Spartans could make neither head nor tail of the reply.

'In Tegea, on the smooth plain of Arcadia,
There is a place where two winds are forced to blow.
Where strike rebounds to strike, to lay woe upon woe.
There life-giving Earth covers Agamemnon's son.
Bring him to Sparta, and Tegea's won.'

(Herodotus History 1.67)

The riddle was finally understood by a Spartan called Lichas. He was of the Agathoergi, one of the leaders of a group of 300 picked Spartan youths whom the Ephors used as the enforcers of their edicts. Once they had served their term, the Agathoergi often went abroad as diplomat-spies representing Spartan interests. While in Tegea, Lichas had reason to visit a blacksmith and in the course of a convivial conversation the Spartan discovered that the smith had been digging a well in his outer courtyard. While doing so the smith had unearthed a massive coffin seven cubits long.

Depending on which of the many ancient variations on the theme of 'cubit' was used by the blacksmith, this was a coffin between ten and twelve feet in length. It was the belief of the classical Greeks that their forebears of the Heroic Age had been larger than themselves (though from the skeletons of Bronze Age Greeks it seems that they were actually shorter). Lichas now started to put it all together.

According to myth, Agamemnon's son was Orestes. That part of the oracle at least was straightforward, and the only reason the priestess had not said so was because she was constrained to speak in iambic sextameters and 'Orestes' lacked the requisite number of syllables. Now it became clear that the 'two winds' were forced from the smithy's bellows, and the hammer rebounded from striking the anvil where woe-bearing weapons were forged. Lichas had found the place mentioned in the oracle. Anxiously he enquired what had become of the coffin. The blacksmith replied that, after having opened the thing to check if the skeleton within was as large as the exterior indicated (it was), he had re-interred it.

A month or so later Lichas returned to the smithy. He sadly informed the owner that he had just been exiled from his native Sparta. Deprived of the income from his *kleros*, he was constrained to make his own way in the world. His previous encounter had convinced Lichas that it was a blacksmith's life for him, and he offered the current occupant of the smithy an exorbitant sum of money to sell the place and – most importantly – everything in it. Barely had the delighted blacksmith departed with his gains than Lichas unpacked his shovels and set to it in the back courtyard. It was not long before the mortal remains of Orestes were on their way to Sparta.

The crucial thing about this mildly ridiculous story is not whether it was true, but whether the Spartans – and just as importantly, the Tegeans – believed it. It was not uncommon for the gods to set these sort of victory conditions. According to myth, the Greeks in the Trojan War had to come up with a particular statue of Athena and the arrows of Hercules before they could capture Troy. Therefore it was not a great stretch to believe that once the Spartans had fulfilled the divine requirement that they take possession of the bones of Orestes, the capture of Tegea would follow. Because both Spartans and Tegeans believed this, morale soared on the Spartan side and plummeted on the Tegean. Thereafter the Tegeans began to lose military actions as regularly as they had previously been successful.

The Peloponnesian League

Fortunately for Tegea, the Spartans had taken the lessons of their previous setbacks to heart. They had realized that absorbing Tegea would probably be one mouthful too many, even for a state with the Spartan appetite for conquest. Furthermore, if relatively tiny Tegea had proven so tough, then subjugating the rest of Arcadia and the entire Argolid was quite certainly beyond Sparta's powers.

Therefore Tegea was offered an alternative – to become a founder member of what later became known as the Peloponnesian League. We have some details of the treaty, because Plutarch indirectly mentions them in his *Moralia*.

> 'When the Lacedaemonians made peace with the Tegeans they signed a treaty, and jointly raised a stele on the banks of the river Alpheus. The Tegeans were to expel Messenian refugees from their lands … those Tegeans who had aided Sparta were not to be executed.'
>
> Plut *Mor* 292B)

We can guess at the further terms of the treaty from the subsequent behaviour of the Tegeans and from the terms offered other members of the League (such as the treaty with Olynthus preserved in Xenophon's Hellenica 5.3.26) Basically, the Tegeans were to contribute men to any military action the Spartans felt necessary. In turn the Spartans agreed to defend Tegea if the *polis* was attacked by any other state. It also appears that the Spartans took over the Tegean foreign policy, since thereafter the Tegeans showed no initiatives in that respect on their own.

We should also note that 'League' is not really an appropriate term for this system, which was more accurately known in antiquity as 'The Spartans and their allies'. This is because the relationships between the Spartans and League members were strictly bilateral – each state had an alliance with Sparta alone, not with other League members. Meetings of the League were called at the Spartan behest, and votes of the League were not binding on Sparta. Nevertheless, the 'League' offered one powerful incentive. Members were guaranteed Spartan protection against aggressors. Given that Argos, and on occasion Corinth, could get remarkably aggressive, there can be no doubt that for every member coerced into the League by Spartan military pressure there was another which voluntarily signed up to the lesser of two evils.

Sparta gained several advantages from the creation of the League. The first was tactical, in that Sparta immediately gained a free expansion of the city's military force. While Sparta was only required to assist allies suffering from aggression, those states were compelled to supply troops to Sparta – at no cost to the Spartans – even when Sparta was being aggressive. As mentioned earlier, this allowed the Spartans to put a mass of allies to blunt the enemy force at the left and centre while they concentrated of demolishing the enemies on the right wing, which is where they invariably stationed themselves. Having broken the line in front of them, the Spartans would then wheel and chew through the rest of the enemy army from the flank.

The second advantage was propaganda. Tegea was Arcadian, and the Spartan kings used their alleged descent from Hercules to stress that they were Achaean rather than Dorian, and therefore proper custodians of the bones of Orestes. This gave a less Dorian flavour to the alliance which made it easier for non-Dorian states to sign up. Once several of these had done so – willingly or unwillingly – the Peloponnesian League was seen as a genuinely multi-ethnic organization.

The final advantage was political. With many Arcadian states now politically aligned with Sparta through the League, and others cowed by the threat of the power of the League being turned upon them, the chances of the Arcadians interfering in Messenia was greatly reduced. In the Argolid, the power of Argos was balanced by the League. Argos naturally wanted nothing to do with membership, but it had to tread lightly to prevent other cities from joining up, and even the most chauvinistic Argive had to confess that the creation of the League had tipped the balance of power in Sparta's favour. Not that this would prevent Argos from testing the limits of that power on numerous future occasions, but the chances of Argos now invading Laconia had become remote. Sparta was now the leading power not only in the Peloponnese but in Greece as a whole, and it had the League to thank for this.

Chilon

The creation of the League required a far greater degree of foresight and diplomacy than Sparta had heretofore exercised. Ancient tradition ascribes this policy to one man – and many modern historians agree. (eg. Conrad Stibbe in *Das Andere Sparta* Mainz: 1996) The ancient Greeks had a sort of game by which they compiled things in lists of seven (such as the Seven Wonders of the World). Another list was of the 'seven sages' – the wisest men in Greece. Given each city's bias, it is unsurprising that they came up with a total of seventeen candidates on different lists. However two names feature on every list we have today: Solon the Athenian, and Chilon the Spartan.

That Solon should feature is unsurprising. He was a great law-giver, and the Athenians were relentless at self-promotion, so Solon's achievements were widely known and respected. Chilon is more surprising. The Spartans were a more secretive nation, and their emphasis on teamwork and group-think meant that it was rare for an individual's merit to be acknowledged, no matter how outstanding that individual. That he overcame these obstacles to fame makes Chilon truly exceptional.

Chilon was an Ephor, and it is generally agreed that it was he who increased the power of the Ephorate to make it almost on a par with the Kings'. Certainly while he was Ephor, Chilon set the pace in legislation and dictated Spartan policy, of which the creation of the Peloponnesian League was the most foresighted development. We also hear that Chilon was worried about the strategic threat posed by the island of Kythera. 'I wish it had never existed, or, since it does exist I wish it existed at the bottom of the sea.' The island is just off the tip of Cape Malea and it was a convenient naval base for anyone planning a strike at Laconia.

This sort of strategic thinking shows that at the time of Chilon Sparta was taking a greater interest in foreign policy. With the newly-acquired heft of the Peloponnesian League behind it, Sparta began interfering in the politics of other Greek cities. Perhaps because of their bruising experience with Pheidon, tyrant of Argos, the Spartans decided that tyrants were a bad thing. 'It's a fortunate tyrant who dies in his own bed from natural causes', Chilon once commented (*Letter to Periander*, Diog. Laert. Chilon 4).

The Spartans were instrumental in the overthrow of tyrants in Sikyon and Corinth, and over the following centuries showed a strong preference that the cities which they dominated should be ruled by aristocratic oligarchies. Despite being nominally a democracy itself, Sparta was deeply suspicious of this form of government and used its influence to suppress this wherever possible.

Chilon was also a poet, though none of his verses has survived intact. If a fragment in Diogenes Laertius is any guide, his poetry had a strong moralizing bent.

'A whetstone hard is the best test for gold,
This proof of purity is sure,
And for us to know their purity of mind,
Gold itself is the test of men.'

Diog Laert. Chilon 2.

Up to this point Spartan involvement in matters outside Greece had been minimal. Indeed, the nation's attention had been largely focussed on parochial matters within the Peloponnese. 'In external relations, they [the Spartans] kept entirely aloof from non-Greeks', remarks Herodotus. However, once Sparta had come to be seen as the leading power in Greece, other nations started to pay attention to Sparta. One such nation was Lydia, a powerful kingdom in Asia Minor. Lydia was cultured – indeed so much so that the Lydians could justifiably claim to be more civilized than contemporary Greeks, having for example come up with the innovation of coinage which was only now being adopted by forward-thinking Greek states.

Lydia was rich – so rich that from that time until today the wealth of its king has been proverbial – to be as rich as Croesus remains an aspiration for many. However, for all the blessings that providence had showered on his state, Croesus was uneasy. The cause of his unease lay to the east, where a new power had arisen from the Medean desert that threatened to become even greater than the fallen empires of Assyria and Babylon. This was Persia, and Croesus felt reasonably sure that it would be a good idea to crush the aspiring Persian Empire before it properly got started. To this end, Croesus asked the Spartans for an alliance, and flattered, the Spartans agreed. The good feeling between the two nations was cemented by a gift from Croesus. The Spartans had wanted gold for a statue they wished to dedicate to Apollo and they had come to Lydia to purchase that gold. Croesus let them have it as a gift.

With his western flank secure, Croesus consulted the Oracle

at Delphi to ask whether attacking Persia was a good idea. In one of its most famous pronouncements, the Oracle responded that by going to war with Persia, Croesus would destroy a great nation. As ever, the Oracle was infallible, if only one interpreted the words correctly. As Croesus fled the remains of his burning palace in Sardis, it became clear that the great nation he had destroyed was his own. Persia conquered Lydia, and would soon go on to conquer Egypt and the rest of Asia Minor.

While Persia would later be massively influential in Spartan foreign affairs, this first toe-dip into the waters of international diplomacy was of only peripheral concern to the Spartans. They were unable to do much for Croesus because they were once again deeply involved in matters in their own backyard of the Peloponnese.

However, before we turn to this, there is a footnote to the Lydian alliance which is worth noting because it tells us much about the Spartans abroad. As a gift to Croesus, the Spartans...

'… Made a massive bronze vase, with carvings of animals around the outer rim. This was large enough to hold 300 amphorae. They wished to give it to Croesus as thanks for his generosity toward them. The vase never reached Sardis.

There are two very different explanations of what went wrong. The Lacedaemonian story is that while the vase was on its way towards Sardis, the people of [the island of] Samos discovered this treasure was en route. So they put to sea in their warships and captured it.

According to the Samians, the Spartans bearing the vase reached them and discovered that Sardis had already fallen and Croesus was captured [by the Persians]. Therefore they sold the vase to some private individuals who dedicated it in the temple of Hera. The Samians accused the Spartans of having made up the story of the robbery to explain why the vase was not with them when they came home. Such, then, was the fate of the vase.'

Herodotus *History* 1.

Arguably, the misappropriation of the vase was a natural consequence of teaching Spartan boys to use their initiative and to regard a successful theft as a laudable achievement. Or

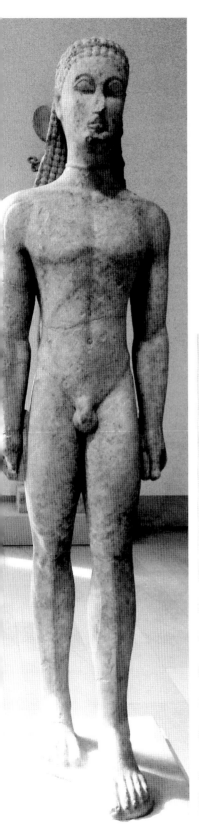

A 'kuros' style statue from archaic
Greece, which shows the strong
influence of Egypt on early Greek art.
(*Photo by P. Matyszak, Met. Mus. of Art, NY*)

A vase from the Archaic era in Greece,
which reflects the importance of horses and
chariots in both aristocratic culture and warfare.
(*Photo by P. Matyszak, Met. Mus. of Art, NY*)

The Taygetos massif as seen from the remains of buildings on the Spartan Acropolis. (*Courtesy of Jackie Whalen*)

A view of the Menelaion, Sparta's Mycenaean-era settlement, looking south-west towards the Eurotas River. (*Courtesy of Jackie Whalen*)

A statuette of a Greek warrior of the archaic period. Note the stylistic resemblance to the 'kuros' statue on page 1. (*Photo by P. Matyszak*)

Another view of the Menelaion from the south side looking west across the Eurotas valley. (*Courtesy of Jackie Whalen*)

The lyre was the principal musical instrument of the classical era. Professional lyricists were highly paid, but – outside Sparta – every well-bor[n] Greek was expected to have a degree of proficiency.

A view of the Taygetos Rang[e] from the Messenian side. Th[is] was less precipitous than th[e] approach from Sparta, whic[h] shows how great a barri[er] the massif was to traveller[s]. (*Courtesy of Jackie Whale[n]*)

A girl at exercise. At knee length this girl's dress is very modest by Spartan standards. The usual attire led to Spartan maidens being nicknamed 'thigh-flashers' by the rest of Greece. (*Photo by P. Matyszak*)

The Temple of Hera in Sparta. Hera was the goddess of wedlock, even with the rather eccentric form of the institution practiced by the Spartans. (*Courtesy of Jackie Whalen*)

A typical armour panoply of the period included the Corinthian helmet and bell cuirass shown here. The helmet was often fitted with a crest to make the wearer seem even more formidable. (*Photo by P. Matyszak*)

Sunset on the Laconian Gulf. On the right is the island of Kythera, which gave security-minded Spartan kings many sleepless nights. (*Courtesy of Jackie Whalen*)

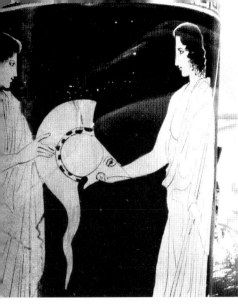

A mother passes a helmet to her son on this red-figure vase. Spartan women appear to have been as committed as their menfolk to the nation's warrior ethos. (*Photo by P. Matyszak, Met. Mus. of Art, NY*)

The warrior on this red-figure vase models his linothorax cuirass for an admiring audience. The social importance of having a good panoply made appearance almost as important as function for the average Spartiate. (*Photo by P. Matyszak*)

This view of the landscape from Delphi shows yet again how little of the Greek mainland was suitable for settlement and agriculture. (*Courtesy of Mark Bretherton*)

A modern statue at Thermopylae commemorates the moment when, in response to a Persian demand that they give up their weapons, the Spartans replied *molon labe* (come and take them). (*Courtesy of Jackie Whalen*)

The pass at Thermopylae toda Changes in the coastline mean that th shore is now well to the right, but in th classical era the gap between mountain and sea was around a hundred metre (*Courtesy of Jackie Whale.*)

ΜΟΛΩΝ ΛΑΒΕ

perhaps the Samians really were a bunch of pirates. However, we should note this was far from the last case of similarly suspicious behaviour by Spartans when their Ephors were far away.

The Spartans were far less concerned with the fate of the vase than with the fate of Thyraea. This small city dominated the eastern coastal strip of the lower Peloponnese. The Spartans were keen to occupy this, not least because doing so would deny the Argives access to Kythera, the island which was currently giving Chilon nightmares.

Confident in their new-found military ability, the Spartans boldly marched onto the plain of Thyraea and 'invited' the folk of the city there to join the Spartan polity. Before the Thyraeans accepted an offer they could not refuse, the Argives mustered an army and drew this up to challenge the Spartan occupation. At this point one of the more bizarre episodes of military history took place. The Argives were somewhat worried about the Corinthians, and the Spartans were still uncertain as to what extent their army might be needed to help Croesus, so both sides were reluctant to suffer the casualties that a full-scale battle would entail. Therefore after some to-and-fro movement by heralds, the armies agreed that each side would select 300 of their finest warriors to represent them. These picked men would fight it out in place of their respective armies, and the losing side would abide by the result just as if a full-scale battle had taken place.

The result was the famous 'Battle of the Champions', usually dated to 546 BC. The armies withdrew in order to prevent spectators from getting over-excited and joining the affray. The terms of the combat were brutally simple. The champions would fight until everyone on the opposing side was dead. Whoever was alive at the end would be victorious.

What followed was a grim and bloody struggle which ended after nightfall with 597 dead. Of these 299 were Spartan casualties while the Argives had two men left standing. Believing that they were the only survivors of the battle, the exhausted pair staggered off to bring the glad news to their army. However, in the darkness they had overlooked one wounded Spartan, either because the Spartan was playing dead, or because his wounds had rendered him so deeply unconscious that he appeared dead.

When he came to and found himself alone and in apparent possession of the battlefield, Othryades the Spartan did as was traditional for those who held the field after a battle. That is, he stripped the armour off a corpse, and took it to build a trophy. A 'trophy' consisted of armour and weapons from the side which had come second, mounted on a tree stump and displaying to the world that the former owner of the armour had lost the battle.

When the two armies returned, the Argives insisted that they had won, because their men were the last ones left standing. The Spartans loftily replied that the pair had fled the battlefield, leaving behind a lone Spartan who therefore counted as having won the day. The argument turned to quarrelling, the quarrelling to blows and the blows to the full-scale battle that both sides had wanted to avoid. At least this time there was no dispute as to who had won. Though both sides suffered heavy casualties, the Spartans defeated the Argives and thereafter took possession of Thyraea and points south, including Kythera.

There was one odd cultural side-effect of this incident. Herodotus notes:

> 'Up until now, it had been the Argive custom for men to wear their hair long. Now they cropped their hair and vowed that no man should wear his hair long, nor any woman wear gold, until Thyraea had been recovered. They reinforced this vow with a law to that effect, and a curse upon anyone who broke it. In response the Spartans, who had heretofore cut their hair short decided to wear it long, as indeed they have done ever since, up to the present day.'
>
> Herodotus *History* 1.82

A final note shows how Sparta's warrior culture was becoming entrenched. Othryades, the Spartan survivor, was ashamed that he had contrived to live while all his comrades had bravely died in battle. He later returned to the place where they had fallen and there he killed himself.

Chapter Eight

Cleomenes I – Sparta's 'Mad' King

Almost everything about the career of Cleomenes I of Sparta is exceptional, often to the point of being bizarre. This includes the circumstances surrounding his conception and birth.

The father of Cleomenes I was King Anaxandrias II (560-c.520 BC), a highly successful king of the Agiad line. To date we have avoided the complex family lives and succession struggles of the Spartan royal families, other than to note that once the historical record becomes more detailed, the regular reigns and father-son succession of king lists from earlier eras becomes considerably more complex. King Anaxandrias and his successors are a good example of this.

Sparta had a relaxed attitude to close-kin marriages, even allowing the marriage of uterine half-siblings (those with the same mother but different fathers – Philo *On Special Laws* 3.4.22). Therefore no-one found it particularly odd that Anaxandrias had chosen to marry his own niece. However, the fact that Anaxandrias was incapable of fathering children on his sister's daughter caused considerable concern in the city.

Since at least the time of Chilon the Ephors had possessed the power to call their kings to account, and they did so on this occasion. Anaxandrias was summoned by the Ephors and told that he had to divorce his barren wife forthwith. The Ephors had a substitute wife lined up – by some accounts a grand-daughter of Chilon himself. This also is none too surprising, because Spartan women – or at least their families – were aggressively hypergamous. That is, daughters tended to marry as high-ranking or powerful a man as possible, and given that Spartan women could and did inherit property, this meant that much of Sparta's assets began to accumulate with a relatively small group of women. It was therefore logical that the family of Chilon should try immediately to leverage the great Ephor's power and prestige into an advantageous marriage for his female descendants. The infertility of Anaxandrias' current wife allowed them this opportunity. (Detailed discussion on Spartan hypergamy can be found in Powell, A. *Classical Sparta* Routledge 2014 edition, p92ff)

The problem was that Anaxandrias loved his niece and had no intention of divorcing her. He informed the Ephors that she had done nothing wrong, and threatened to force a constitutional crisis by defiantly remaining married. A hasty compromise was worked out. If Anaxandrias insisted on being married to his niece, the Ephors would permit this, but only on condition that Anaxandrias contracted a second, bigamous marriage to the woman they had selected from Chilon's family.

The intention was to get the Agiad line breeding again, and in this the Ephors were certainly successful. Hardly had Anaxandrias conceived a child on his second wife than the first became pregnant. This sudden burst of fertility caused deep suspicion among the family of Chilon and their faction. The suspicion was that Anaxandrias' wife was faking a pregnancy to invalidate the King's second marriage. Therefore the unfortunate woman was watched day and night, and she even gave birth with a monitor present to carefully check that the child had come from her womb. He did, and after a careful inspection by the Ephors the boy was accepted and named Doreius. By way of proving the child's conception was no aberration, the suddenly fertile niece pumped out two more children in quick succession – Leonidas and Cleombrotus.

While this dynastic surge by the niece was not in vain, the family of Chilon argued successfully that the first born of Anaxandrias' sons was the rightful heir to the Agiad crown. That child was Cleomenes, son of Anaxandrias' second wife. (Incidentally it tells us something of the contemporary attitude to women that neither of the female protagonists is named by our sources – despite their intimate involvement with the story, both remain anonymous battery hens. How they felt about events and each other no-one has bothered to record.)

Not unexpectedly Doreius, the first-born son of wife number one was not greatly satisfied with this decision, especially because, even as a youth Cleomenes had already demonstrated a remarkably eccentric bent. That the Spartans had chosen this erratic young scion of an irregular marriage over the clearly level-headed son of the previous king's 'proper' spouse so offended the unsuccessful heir that Doreius stormed out of the city to make a life – and premature death – for himself as a military adventurer in Magna Graecia (the Greek cities of Italy and Sicily).

Cleomenes came to the throne in 520 BC (this date is uncertain and may have been 519 or even 518). By this time Sparta's grip on the Peloponnese had tightened. Skilful diplomacy had allied Corinth with Sparta, while the influence of the League and a bout of misplaced Argive aggression had switched the alliance of most Arcadian tribes from Argos to Sparta. As a result, Argos was dangerously isolated and looking for support from states further north, especially Athens and Thebes. This support was grudging if given at all, for such was Sparta's growing power that no-one in Greece was eager to offend the Spartans.

Sparta had even flirted with naval activity in the late sixth century. At this point the city came into unexpected possession of a fleet of some forty warships. These came from the tyrant Polycrates of Samos, who was having trouble with internal dissent. Polycrates noted that the new style of warship dominating the Aegean Sea was the trireme. Though fast and powerful, these ships needed a lot of manpower – a minimum of 200 men per ship. It occurred to Polycrates that if he were to stuff each ship in the fleet with his political opponents, then send them against the Persians, all it would take was one major defeat for 8000 of his problems to end up at the bottom of the ocean.

So the ships were outfitted and sent off to battle, with a secret messenger sent ahead warning the Persians where and when to expect them. However, the ship's crews had their own agenda. They put to sea, but rather than sail against the Persians, the dissidents promptly defected to Sparta. Sparta and Corinth combined forces in an attempt to use the fleet to overthrow the Samian tyrant, but Polycrates was too well entrenched behind his defences. After trying for over a month to find a way through the Spartans gave up and went home. Though the expedition had been unsuccessful, Sparta had demonstrated its enmity to tyranny and the city's ever-increasing reach. What became of the dissident fleet is unknown, but as a propaganda device, the Spartans seemed satisfied with the use they had made of it.

Indeed, in a burst of hubris, the Spartans even sent a messenger to the Persian King of Kings telling him to leave the Greek cities of Asia Minor alone or suffer the consequences. It is quite possible that up to this point the Persian King had never even heard of Sparta, and certainly the warning was disregarded. Persia went on to conquer the Greek cities of Ionia, outraging the Athenians who regarded the people of these cities as their kin. It was from this point onward that Persia began to play an ever-increasing role in Greek affairs. However, for all the severe admonishment that they had given the Persian juggernaut, cautious, inward-looking Sparta was slow to get involved.

Even Cleomenes, for all that he intended to be a dynamic proactive ruler, especially in foreign affairs, realized that Persia represented a challenge out of all proportion to the other cities of Greece. He did, early in his reign, entertain an exile from Miletus who (according to Herodotus *History* 5.49) came close to persuading Cleomenes that he should attempt the invasion and conquest of Persia. Young Cleomenes was at first eager, until he asked how long it would take an army to march from the coast to the Persian capital of Susa. He was informed that the feat could be accomplished within three months by a suitably motivated army with a clear passage.

This was the first intimation of the sheer scale of Persia's vast empire, and it came as something of a shock to a King who was accustomed to being able to send a message to Argos at breakfast with the expectation of being able to read the reply at supper the following day. Given that the helots of Messenia would be at the throats of their Spartan overlords within a week of the army setting off on such an extended mission, Cleomenes took no further interest in the proposal. (This story is told twice, with a different petitioner from Ionia in each case. Both times Cleomenes was offered extravagant bribes, but refused them at the urging of his daughter Gorgo.)

Athens

Almost ten years went by before the first chance arose to flex some serious diplomatic muscle. This opportunity came in 510, when Cleomenes had the chance to interfere with the internal affairs of Athens.

In the late sixth century BC, Athens was ruled by a tyrant. As previously mentioned, there need be nothing particularly tyrannical about a 'tyrant'. All that a man needed to gain the title in late Archaic Greece was that he had come to power irregularly, usually by overthrowing the established dynasty. Athens did not have an established dynasty, but the father of the current tyrant had certainly come to power in an irregular fashion. This man was called Psistratus. His colourful career had included multiple ejections from the city each followed by a triumphant return. For one return, Pisistratus found a large girl of striking appearance and dressed her as Athena, patron Goddess of Athens. He then set the girl in a chariot, and entered the city announcing that Athena herself wanted him to be in charge.

It is more probable that the Athenian people acquiesced in this particular coup more out of dissatisfaction with their current rulers than through unsophisticated superstition. Though he was forced from power once more, the persevering tyrant forced himself back into power mainly with the help of mercenaries hired for the purpose.

Despite this violent seizure of power it appears that most Athenians were relatively satisfied with Psistratus, who does indeed appear to have ruled competently and untyranically. Herodotus allows that he governed 'fairly and well' (Herodotus *History* 1.59). The main body of the tyrant's support came from the lower classes whom Psistratus championed against the aristocracy. A large public works programme helped stimulate the Athenian economy, and this included an aqueduct which relieved citizens of their dependence on the River Eridanos. This river flowed through the city, becoming increasingly a mixture of refuse bin and sewer as it went along. Certainly the water was a severe health hazard by the time it exited the walls once more.

Unlike most tyrants, Psistratus died in bed after arranging a peaceful succession of power to his two sons. That is where things started to go wrong. One son was assassinated (for reasons only partly to do with politics) and the other became a paranoid dictator. This gave opponents of the tyrant the opportunity they had been looking for. Leading the anti-Pisistratid movement were an aristocratic family called the Alcmaeonids (the most famous son of this clan was Pericles, born two generations later).

The Alcmaeonids called on Sparta to relieve Athens of the yoke of the tyrant, just as Sparta had done previously in Sikyon and Corinth. Cleomenes was eager to get involved, but the cautious Ephors and Gerousia urged him to first consult the Pythia at Delphi. As it happened, the Oracle was prepared to totally – and for once unambiguously – endorse the Spartan proposal to liberate Athens. The cynical Herodotus suggests that this might have something to do with members of the Alcmaeonid clan who had been in exile in Delphi for a while, and who had both built a lavish temple and otherwise strewn money about with lavish abandon. In short, the Oracle was bribed.

Nevertheless, even with 'divine' endorsement, the first Spartan attempt was a failure. The Athenian tyrant had good intelligence of Cleomenes' plans, and not trusting his own people to resist a liberation attempt, he had borrowed over 1,000 cavalry from nearby Thessaly. The Spartan force was not expecting to face so many horsemen and was taken by surprise. The leader of the expedition was killed and the rest driven back to their ships. The survivors of the expedition then sailed back to Sparta in ignominious retreat.

The Spartan establishment might not have been totally behind the first expedition of Cleomenes, but once this was thrown back, the state had no choice but to throw its full support behind a further attempt. By now the Spartans had too much invested in their image as a major military power to be seen to fail so publicly. The second expedition to Athens was led by Cleomenes himself, and it went by land – partly to demonstrate that the Spartan army could march wherever it pleased.

This time the Spartans were ready for the Thessalian cavalrymen and brushed them aside while barely pausing on their march to Athens. The Psistratids were ready for the assault. They had sent their families to safety and were themselves holed up on the Athenian Acropolis with abundant supplies of food and water. This left Cleomenes somewhat nonplussed, for siege warfare in that era was a primitive affair which usually involved a lot of patience on one side and careful rationing on the other. Starving the Psistratids out of the Acropolis would take a great deal more time than the Spartans had budgeted for. Consequently, like the first, this second expedition might have failed ignominiously if the gods had not proven that they were, after all, on the Spartan side. Quite by chance, the Spartans intercepted the families of the Psistratid leaders in their attempt to flee from Attica. Though they themselves were safe on the Acropolis, the Psistratid menfolk now had their wives and children in Spartan hands. Negotiations followed.

In the end, the Psistratids agreed to depart from Athens into exile. Hippias, the former tyrant, chose to exile himself not just from Athens, but also from Greece. He went to Persia and there petitioned the Persian king to restore him to power in Athens as a Persian vassal. (As time went on, and the Athenians made themselves increasingly obnoxious to the Persian King, this offer was eventually taken seriously.)

The aristocratic Alcmaeonids of Athens had achieved their goal and overthrown their Pisistratid rivals. They immediately took charge of the restored government, and made it plain to Cleomenes that all the Spartans were going to get from their effort and sacrifice were cool thanks and cordial wishes for a safe trip back to Sparta. Cleomenes himself appears to have enjoyed the enthusiastic hospitality of the wife of Isagoras, another leading Athenian aristocrat (there was something of a scandal about this), and to have buffed up his credentials as an Achaean by visiting a temple in Athens from which Dorians were banned. (As mentioned on p.14).

Nevertheless, the ingratitude of the Alcmaeonids left Cleomenes feeling considerably miffed. While he had not expected to set up a puppet government, he had at least hoped for an administration that was sympathetic toward Sparta's interests. Since the Alcmaeonids seemed bent instead on further democratizing a state that was, from a Spartan viewpoint, far too democratic already, Cleomenes was more than ready to listen to the complaints of Isagoras when that worthy was expelled from Athens. Consequently, a few years after Cleomenes had marched on Athens to depose Hippias the Tyrant, he was marching back again to impose Isagoras the Tyrant on the Athenians. Contemporary Greeks were quick to point out the inconsistency, which did much to damage Sparta's reputation as a high-minded liberator.

The Alcmaeonids who did not get out of town before

Cleomenes arrived were thrown out immediately afterwards, for Isagoras had supplied the King with a list of 700 families whom he considered hostile. This represented a good proportion of the Athenian populace, and rather embittered the rest. However, this was as nothing compared to the indignation which greeted Cleomenes when he attempted to dismantle the Athenians' prized and hard-won democratic institutions and set up in their place the sort of repressive oligarchy that was the preferred Spartan form of government.

A popular uprising followed. Cleomenes had not the men to take on the entire Athenian people, and had to retreat to the Acropolis. It is doubtful that he appreciated the irony of being holed up in the Athenian Acropolis by those wanting to overthrow the current regime, especially as, unlike the Psistratids before him, Cleomenes had neglected to lay in any supplies. Once again a withdrawal from the Acropolis was negotiated with the besiegers, and Cleomenes and his men left Attica with their tails between their legs and thoughts of revenge in their hearts. Currently Cleomenes' record in Attica was two strikes out of three, and a city which had gone from friendly neutrality to cold hostility. The Ephors and Gerousia were unimpressed.

Cleomenes was determined to make Athens pay for his discomfiture, and he promptly began to assemble allies from the Peloponnesian League and a formidable army for the purpose. As well as League members, the vengeful king collected troops from a sympathetic Corinth, and further reinforcements from Chalcis and Boeotia, as these states saw the chance for some opportunistic pillaging. The general belief was that when faced with this large combined force, the Athenians would knuckle under and meekly accept the tyranny of Isagoras. Sparta would accept a large indemnity to soothe the state's wounded pride, and share this among the allies. Isagoras would be installed as the Spartan sock puppet that the Alcmaeonids had refused to be, and back in Sparta, the stock of Cleomenes would soar.

It was a great script, but unfortunately for Cleomenes the Athenians appeared not to have read it. Far from being deterred, the Athenians were provoked by the invasion. The army they mustered in response reminded their startled opponents that Attica was one of the largest and most populous states in Greece.

Seeing that the Athenians were ready and willing to do battle, the Corinthian contingent developed severely cold feet. A show of force was one thing, but the Corinthians were not prepared to actually fight and die just to re-inflate the ego of Cleomenes. They informed the outraged Spartan king that they wanted to go home.

Things unravelled quickly after that. The co-regent with Cleomenes, the Eurypontid king Demaratus, maintained that the Corinthians had a point, and he too saw no point in risking the Spartan army in an unnecessary battle. This was enough for the League members, some of whom had not wanted to be there in the first place. They had sworn to obey the Spartans in war, but when Sparta's leaders disagreed, they felt that they had a choice of which Spartan to obey. They voted for Demaratus, and they voted with their feet. Within a short time the huge and intimidating force assembled by Cleomenes had melted away like springtime snow.

This almost disappointed the Athenians who had taken the field charged up for battle, only to have the opposing army dissolve in front of them. Fortunately, the Boeotian contingent could not go far because Boeotia was next door to Attica. Therefore the Athenians fell upon the Boeotians and the Chalcidians who had stuck with them for the illusion of safety, and won a resounding victory. It was a triumph which solidified support for the fledgling Athenian democracy by showing what the united Athenian people could achieve.

In Sparta, apart from pushing the stock of Cleomenes to record lows, the disagreement of the two kings on the battlefield led to a constitutional amendment. The Ephors ruled that henceforth only one king would lead the army to war. That way, the Spartan army would have a unified command which would avoid a repeat of the recent embarrassment, and Sparta would have a king in reserve if something went horribly wrong and the army and its leaders were slain.

Ionia

Ionian Greece was that part of the Greek world which took up the Aegean Sea and the western coast of Asia Minor. It was called Ionia because most of the peoples were of the Ionian tribe, and it was believed by contemporary Greeks that the Ionian cities of the east were founded by refugees who had been displaced from the Greek mainland by invading Dorians during the Dark Ages.

Modern archaeology has shown that this picture is only partly correct, because some Ionian cities pre-date the Dark Ages, but the belief of the classical Greeks that the Ionians had fled Dorian aggression is nevertheless important. This is because the belief engendered a degree of suspicion and antipathy between these two major ethnic groups which was to prove problematic when Greece as a whole was faced with a common threat.

This threat was Persia, the power which had arisen in the lands east of the Tigris River and which had, under a succession of capable rulers, expanded steadily westward, reaching the shores of the Mediterranean in the mid-sixth century BC. As described (p.94) the Persians had taken out the rich and prosperous kingdom of Lydia. Thereafter, they had conquered Egypt, a country which had been governed by its own rulers for the previous 2500 years. With Lydia and Egypt absorbed by the Persian Empire, the Greek cities of Asia Minor and the eastern Aegean barely counted as a mopping-up operation, not least because their lack of political unity meant that the cities were easily picked off one by one.

It has to be said that the Persians were generally tolerant and easy-going rulers. They allowed the Greek cities to rule themselves, though they generally followed the standard sixth century practice of installing tyrants to do the actual ruling. However, the Greeks were accustomed to the total independence of each *polis*, and bitterly resented their Persian overlords. Eventually they rose in rebellion, inspired paradoxically enough by one of the very tyrants the Persians had installed. This tyrant had bungled a military operation, and fearful of being replaced, he had inspired his people to rise in a rebellion which soon became a general conflagration.

Ionians themselves, the Athenians considered themselves the natural leaders of the Ionian Greeks and they quickly put themselves at the forefront of the rebellion. In 498 BC a combined force of Athenians and Ionian rebels marched on the Persian provincial capital of Sardis, and pillaged and burned the city. This was certainly enough to get the attention of the Persian King of Kings, Darayavahus, the man known to western historians as Darius I (550- 486 BC). Darius now turned his attention westward, and as well as ordering his generals to suppress the revolt, he ordered them to take an interest in the Greek mainland beyond from whence support for the rebellion had come.

For the next four years the Persians systematically crushed the Ionian rebels. They combined brutal force against any resistance with a surprisingly moderate settlement once that resistance had been overcome. Since tyrants had proven somewhat unsuccessful as rulers, the Persians settled for having the Greek cities governed by oligarchs, and in some cases where the locals insisted, even democracies were tolerated. The Persians started to take an interest in Greek religion and culture, and there was even a degree of intermarriage between the local Greek and Persian nobility.

However, if all was forgiven, it was certainly not forgotten. In fact Darius had delegated a slave to give him a daily reminder, 'Master, do not forget the Athenians'. The Persian king had a score to settle with the mainland Greeks, and he would not be content until he had received their surrender. Accordingly, in the years before 490 BC a series of ambassadors were dispatched to the Greek mainland to demand gifts of earth and water as tokens of submission. One of these was the ambassador whose arrival in Laconia was chronicled in the opening chapter of this book.

The Persian ambassador's timing was not good. He arrived in a city which was still smarting from the debacle of Cleomenes' most recent attempt to subdue the Athenians, and wracked by internal disagreements about who was to blame and what to do about it. The sudden demand that Sparta submit to a foreign power from across the Aegean Sea was, from a Spartan viewpoint, both outré and impertinent. Therefore the Spartans might be excused a degree of impatience in their response. If the Persian ambassador wanted earth and water, he could get them himself. To help him do so, the Spartans threw the unfortunate man down a well. The Athenians also rejected the Persian demand, but more politely.

Argos

Argos, on the other hand, gave the Persians a wary welcome.

This caused some alarm in Sparta which had suspicions enough already about the Argives without having to worry that their city might become the springboard for a joint Persian-Argive invasion of Laconia. Being Spartans, and at that Spartans led by the impetuous King Cleomenes, they decided to get their retaliation in first. Accordingly a Spartan army marched on Argos. The intention appears to have been firstly, to punish the Argives for being sympathetic to the Persians, secondly to show the rest of Greece that whatever had happened recently outside Athens, the Spartans were still to be taken very seriously, and thirdly, if at all possible, to take the Argive army out of the game before it could be used by the Persians against Sparta.

It should be noted that the above sequence is only one interpretation of an obscure and poorly dated series of events. Herodotus, our earliest reporter, wrote fifty years after the event and did not place it in chronological context. Others, including Plutarch and Cicero wrote almost 500 years later, so their interpretation and chronology are also suspect. (A full discussion of the dating problems is given in 'The Battle of Sepeia' by I. Hendriks in Mnemosyne, Fourth Series, Vol. 33, Fasc. 3/4 (1980), pp. 340-346.)

At whatever date the invasion happened, the Spartans arrived in the Argolid in the region of the city of Tiryns, a location mainly famous as the birthplace of the hero Hercules. Here a large Argive army waited to confront the Spartans. The Greek world might have expected another of those bruising, man-to-man struggles in which Spartan hoplite and Argive warrior battled for supremacy, but yet again – as we have seen remarkably often in early Spartan history – the Spartans won by a trick. The nature of that trick is uncertain, for we have two different versions.

In one version, the Argives took their cue from Spartan signals. When Spartan trumpets mustered the army for battle, the Argives mustered also. When the Spartans tried to move right or left, their manoeuvres were mirrored by the Argive army. When Cleomenes ordered his men to stand down, the Argives stood down also. The same happened the next day when the two armies once again faced off against each other. Then Cleomenes gave his army the signal to stand down and have breakfast, so the Argives stood down also. Unfortunately for the breakfasting

Argives, Cleomenes had been watching the Argive imitation tactic and had ordered his men to ignore the command to stand down for the morning meal. The Spartans stayed in their ranks, and once the enemy army had begun to relax, they charged their disorganized opponents and easily routed them.

Unsporting as this may be, Cicero reports an even more dastardly version. According to him, once the two armies came face-to-face, Cleomenes requested a truce of four days to see if a peace deal could be worked out. The Argives agreed, and that night the Spartans fell on the Argive camp and destroyed the unsuspecting and overly-trusting army. When reproachfully asked what had happened to the famous Spartan Code of Honour, Cleomenes replied the truce had only specified four days. No-one had said anything about the nights.

Whichever version one might choose to believe, the upshot of the Battle of Sepeia (as the battle came to be known) was that the Spartans took the Argives by surprise and defeated them. However, his conduct had been up to this point, there can be no doubt that in the aftermath of the battle Cleomenes was totally dishonourable. The remnants of the Argive army took shelter in woodland sacred to the city's eponymous founder. Herodotus takes up the tale:

'Now the treachery of Cleomenes was outright. He had learned from Argive deserters the names of some of those sheltering in the wood. A herald came to the edge of the wood, and called these men by name, saying that they had been ransomed [by friends or family in Argos], and they could now leave the wood in safety. As the men left, one by one, each was cut down as soon as he was out of sight of his comrades. ... Finally, someone in the wood climbed a tree and saw what was happening, and after that no-one else took the offer to leave the sanctuary. Therefore Cleomenes ordered his helots to pile kindling around the wood and set it ablaze.'

Herodotus *History* 6.80

The remainder of the Argive army perished in the blaze, and it appeared that Argos itself was defenceless. Nevertheless, Cleomenes did not take Argos. Far from being inexplicable, this strange conduct by the Spartan King has no less than three separate explanations, depending on whom one asks. The Argives report as follows:

> 'Women have never acted more famously for the public good than in the battle fought against Cleomenes by the Argive women. They were inspired by the poet Telesilla, who is said to have been the daughter of a distinguished family...
>
> When Cleomenes, the Spartan King, killed many Argives (but not the 7777 men that some allege) he marched against the city. The gods inspired the younger women with impulsive courage so that they defended their homeland against the foe. With Telesilla as their commander, they took up arms and - to the amazement of the enemy - defended the city walls. Cleomenes was driven off with heavy casualties.'
>
> Plutarch *Moralia* 245

The Spartans had a different explanation. They believed that the Argive women had bribed Cleomenes to leave their city alone. They put their King on trial for this once he had returned to Laconia. At his trial, Cleomenes offered his own explanation for how he had acted.

Cleomenes told the court that he had been told by the Oracle at Delphi that the gods permitted him to take Argos. However, once he discovered that the sacred woodlands that he had burned down were also called 'Argos' (after the hero to whom the trees were sacred), he was no longer sure that he had divine permission to take the city of Argos as well.

After the battle and the subsequent massacre by fire of the Argive survivors, he had consulted the gods by praying at the temple of Hera. He saw a flame shoot from the breast of a statue of the Goddess, and interpreting this as a sign that he was not to attempt to storm the city, Cleomenes had returned home. This explanation was good enough for the devout Spartans, and Cleomenes was acquitted, but the Ephors may have watched their errant king closely thereafter.

There is also a fourth explanation. The purpose of the Spartan attack was to make sure that Argos could not join with the Persians to launch an attack on Lacedaemonia. Therefore the Spartans were looking to destroy the Argive army rather than to take territory which they would have to hold with an army that – given the tense diplomatic situation – might be needed elsewhere at any moment. Once the army had done its job and taken the Argive army out of the picture, it had returned to Sparta, available for future deployment rather than being bogged down holding the Argolid against a resentful local population and a jealous and suspicious neighbour, as Corinth would doubtless become.

Aegina, Arcadia and death

That the Spartan army would swiftly be needed elsewhere became almost immediately apparent. The island of Aegina lay in the Saronic Gulf not far from Athens, the city which was the island's historic rival. Partly because Athens had rejected the Persian demands for submission, the Aegintians cheerfully gave earth and water to their Persian ambassador. They probably believed that, in alliance with the Persians, they would be able to assault Athens rather as Sparta had feared that Argos and the Persians would assault them.

Cleomenes acted swiftly when news of the island's Persian sympathies reached Sparta. In 491 Sparta's forces were on the island looking to arrest those who had attempted to collaborate with the Persians. The King led the Spartans himself, and rather as had happened in Athens, his particular brand of diplomacy quickly united the entire island against him. The people of the island were well aware of Sparta's military power, and swiftly pointed out that they were not opposing the Spartan state, but one of the Spartan kings – for Demaratus was opposed to the intervention by Cleomenes and was agitating to have him brought home. (Demaratus himself was already in Sparta in accordance with the new edict that the two Kings should not both be outside the city.)

This was the second time that Sparta's allies had used dissent between the Kings to go their own way, and Cleomenes was determined it would be the last. Leaving the people of Aegina to their own devices for the present, Cleomenes headed back to Sparta for a showdown with his arch-rival and co-regent. First though, he had to make a stop at Delphi on order to have a word with the Oracle.

In Sparta, Cleomenes did not attack his fellow King directly. Instead he used a relative of Demaratus called Leotychides. These two kinsfolk had been bitter foes ever since Leotychides had intended to marry a girl and Demaratus had carried her off first. Now, urged by Cleomenes, Leotychides brought a claim before the Gerousia that Demaratus was not of the Eurypontid line and therefore not a legitimate King. Once again we get a brief glimpse into the fact that succession in Sparta was more complex than the king lists make it out to be.

The list says that Demaratus was the son of Ariston. All well and good, but Ariston married the mother of Demaratus soon after her divorce from a previous husband. According to the writ presented by Leotychides, the mother was already pregnant when she remarried, and Leotychides was prepared to give the testimony of a servant that Demaratus was either not Ariston's son, or that the birth was unbelievably premature. Actually, according to the mother herself, Demaratus was born after a seven-month pregnancy, but this was enough to make the Spartans seriously consider the suggestion of Cleomenes that they consult Delphi as to their King's paternity.

Again, the message from Delphi was perfectly clear. Demaratus, declared the Oracle, was not the son of Ariston. Accordingly, Demaratus was deposed and Leotychides was made King in his place. The indignant Demaratus fled from Sparta to Persia where he sought sanctuary with King Darius. Darius welcomed the defector with open arms, and gave him abundant lands and rich estates. Demaratus became the King's advisor on Grecian affairs, and especially on matters pertaining to Sparta – information vital to Darius when he later invaded Greece.

Meanwhile Cleomenes was able to return to Aegina. This time he was able to sort out the place to his satisfaction. He took the leading Persian sympathizers into custody and handed them over to the Athenians. However a scandal was already brewing. Inquiring minds were curious about the stop Cleomenes had made at Delphi after his first, unsuccessful, excursion to Aegina. It will be remembered that the Alcmaeonids of Athens were suspected of having bribed the oracle to gain Spartan support against the Psistratids. So Cleomenes had stopped by on his way home to enquire if the Oracle was for sale. Apparently it was.

Once news got out that the Oracle had been compromised, the authorities at Delphi promptly banished the man Cleomenes had bribed, and stripped the Priestess of her role as the Oracle of Apollo. Meanwhile the Ephors began to consider what to do about Cleomenes, who had disposed of a fellow King by illegitimate means. Cleomenes did not wait for a formal summons to defend the indefensible. He fled Sparta.

Officially, Cleomenes was still the Agiad King of Sparta, and the close-mouthed Spartans were not willing to bruit their dirty laundry abroad. Therefore, when Cleomenes arrived in Arcadia and began to gather an army, the Arcadian allies might have wondered what the Spartans were up to, but they were bound by treaty to supply the men demanded. Something else that might have struck the allies as odd was that Cleomenes insisted on the newly-recruited soldiers swearing to be loyal by the most solemn and dreadful oaths. But the loyalty they swore was to Cleomenes himself rather than to his country.

If the allies were confused, the Spartans were downright alarmed. They sent messengers to Cleomenes assuring him that no action was contemplated in the Delphic bribery scandal. All was forgiven and forgotten, so could Cleomenes please return and resume being King. Cleomenes agreed, and returned to Sparta. Shortly thereafter he was placed in chains, and soon after that he was dead, allegedly by suicide.

Perhaps because their cynical fellow Greeks did not believe this for a moment, the Spartans unbent from their usual code of silence to give more complete details. Cleomenes had always been erratic to the point of eccentricity, and the stress of the Demaratus affair and its Arcadian aftermath had apparently driven the man right over the edge into insanity. Soon after he returned to Sparta, Cleomenes had begun attempting to drive the butt of his staff into the face of whomever he encountered, and the Spartans were forced to place him in protective custody. However, while locked in chains, Cleomenes got hold of a knife.

'Cleomenes took the weapon and set about slashing himself from his shins upwards. Starting from the shin he cut his flesh lengthways to the thigh. From the thigh to the hip he cut to the sides. When he reached his belly, he began cutting it off in strips. And so he died.'

Herodotus *History* 6.75

Oddly enough, the Greeks found this horrible death to be convincing proof of suicide. After all, Cleomenes had certainly destroyed the sacred grove of Argos. He had also played fast and loose with his oath in the battle which preceded that. Above all, Cleomenes had suborned a Priestess of Apollo, and Apollo was well known to lack a sense of humour about such things. After all, the God had once flayed alive the Satyr Marsayas for challenging his skill with the lyre. Was the punishment of Cleomenes much different?

With Cleomenes gone, the Agiad kingship fell to an altogether different character, Cleomenes' half-brother Leonidas. Perhaps, in all this controversy, the gods were looking after Greece after all. The outcome of suicide and tragedy was that it fell to Leonidas rather than the flighty and eccentric Cleomenes to defend Thermopylae at that critical moment when Greece faced conquest and enslavement.

Chapter Nine

The Spartan Army

By the late sixth century, the Spartan army had evolved into a fighting machine which enemies tried to avoid if given the slightest chance. Those who went into battle against the Spartans did so in the expectation that they would lose, and this became a self-fulfilling expectation. The reason for this lies in the manner of fighting employed by Greek hoplite armies.

Hoplites fought 'shield against rounded shield' (as the poet Tyndareus puts it). The name 'hoplite' means something like 'armoured man' and as the name implies, a hoplite in the battle-line was well defended by his panoply. Most casualties in a battle were sustained by the side which broke first and ran away. Once a hoplite was deprived of the protection of the warriors on either side of him, he was easy to kill – especially as a fleeing man usually discarded the large shield which was his principal form of defence.

The problem was that those who were the first to break ranks and run from the battle line had the better chance of survival, because the enemy had first to get through those still standing their ground. On the other hand, those brave souls who remained fighting in a crumbling battle line ended up being captured or killed. Therefore, if the battle line was going to break, those who broke first and fastest were the ones who got out alive.

Naturally, this did not apply to the Spartans, who were indoctrinated from early childhood to prefer death to the dishonour of flight. Any Spartan who did run would have been so ostracised and mocked that life would not be worth living anyway. Therefore those going into battle against the Spartans knew that only one battle line was eventually going to break, and that battle line was theirs.

This would have been true even if the side opposing the Spartans had the same degree of training and skill as the Spartans had, because their side lacked the Spartan motivation to stay in the ranks and fight to the end. However, the reality was that at this time the Spartans were the best-trained and most skilful warriors in Greece, and a sure bet to defeat even twice their number in combat.

Therefore in any army facing the Spartans, those in the battle-line had a tendency to keep looking around as they tried to find the perfect balance between not appearing cowardly and not leaving it too late to run for their lives. This preoccupation tended to be a fatal distraction to men facing a finely-honed and trained killing machine whose components were focussed only on victory or death. Consequently, when up against the Spartans, other hoplites expected to lose, and partly as a result of that expectation, they did.

Only partly, because the other part of the formula for victory lay in the nature of a Spartan warrior. Spartan soldiers made up one of the world's first professional armies. A Spartiate had no other job than to be the best warrior he could be. When he was not training for war, the Spartiate was idle. Farming, trading and handiwork were left to *perioiki*, helots and slaves. The difference between Sparta and Athens is well illustrated by the story of the Spartan visitor to Athens who heard that an Athenian had been prosecuted in the courts for idleness. The Spartan said that he would like to meet this Athenian, who was evidently the only free man in the city.

This does not mean that Spartans were generally lazy. A Spartan's day was spent exercising (it would be disgraceful not to keep up with one's comrades in a forced march), hunting (which counted as sport, not work) or training younger soldiers in military techniques. For example, it was not uncommon for older Spartans to march young men to their dining hall in military formation, train the youths to peel off in squads to their dining tables and then to re-form ranks after eating before they marched off again.

The Panoply

It was also typical of the Spartans that each warrior looked almost identical in similar armour, a red cloak (the red cloak came to be as emblematic for Spartan warriors as the red coat to later British soldiers) and in later years a shield bearing the upside-down V of the Greek letter lambda. 'L' for 'Lacadaemonia'. However,

Spartans of the current era preferred individual panoplies and shields that showed off their particular style and taste. At this time, shield designs were a matter of choice.

Although the Greeks unhelpfully stopped burying their weapons along with dead warriors around the sixth century, archaeologists have been able to keep track of the various changes in style as the fifth century went on. This is thanks to the rise of realistic vase paintings, which frequently portrayed contemporary military scenes. The purchasers of these vases would have been intimately familiar with the kit displayed, and quick to point out where the painter got it wrong. Since vases agree with the few items of gear which have been discovered, these depictions should be considered accurate unless there are indications to the contrary.

Shield – *Aspis*

Since the shield, above all, identified a hoplite warrior we will start our examination of a Spartan panoply with this. The *aspis* – the hoplite shield – is known today as the Argive shield. However, this type of shield did not originate in Argos but among the northern tribes which invaded Greece in the Dark Ages. The same tribes invaded Italy, which is why contemporary warriors there appear to have borne the same shields.

The shield was between 80cm and 100cm wide. It was circular, and had a grip in the middle. Originally this grip was an embedded hand grip, as the Roman shield continued to be. In Greece by the sixth century the hoplite shield grip was designed so that the forearm slipped through it, and the hand actually clasped a band at the side of the shield. Thus the shield not only protected each warrior from throat to knees, but also projected beyond his body to give cover to the man on the warrior's left.

Victorious generals had the habit of dedicating their shields after a successful battle. Therefore enough shields have been retrieved from Delphi, Olympia, and other sacred sites to give us a good idea of their design and manufacture – especially as we frequently see the final product portrayed in detail on Greek vases.

It seems that the original shield was made from strips of wood, preferably a close-grained wood such as oak. These strips were overlaid in different layers, rather like modern plywood, so that they did not split across the grain when struck. A bronze rim was hammered on to the shield, or in some cases the entire shield was faced in a thin layer of bronze. The bronze rim made the shield a useful extempore offensive weapon, as the edge could be slammed into throats or exposed limbs if the opportunity presented itself.

One did not want to over-do the protection afforded by a bronze shield facing, as even a basic shield weighed around 7kg (15.4lbs), and this weight often had to be carried for long periods without a break. Here the rounded shape of the shield was helpful, as reconstructions have shown that it is possible to rest the top part of the rim on the bearer's shoulder and carry much of the burden in this way. Nevertheless, in many cases a bronze rim was deemed sufficient, and the rest of the shield was faced with hardened leather.

In later years, when faced by missile troops, such as the toxophiliac Persians and their hosts of archers, hoplites sometimes attached a wide leather flap to the bottom of the shield to prevent low-flying arrows from damaging their calves and thighs.

The round, sturdy body of a shield made it a convenient stretcher in the aftermath of a battle, and dead warriors were conveyed from the field in this manner. (Hence the Spartan mother's famous injunction to her son – 'Come back with this shield, or on it.')

The Spear – *Doru*

The main offensive weapon of a warrior in the battle line was his spear. This was for stabbing rather than throwing, since it was unmanly for any hoplite, let alone a Spartiate, to face his enemy other than face-to-face. The weapon was around 2.5m (8ft) in length. The shaft was usually of ash and tipped with a broad, leaf-shaped steel blade that was sharpened to a razor edge. The other end also had a smaller sharpened point (the 'lizard-killer') that served as a counter-weight and as an extra spear-point should the working end of the weapon get broken off. It has been theorized that this could also be used to finish off a wounded enemy with a downward stab as the victorious phalanx rolled over him. This seems rather a stretch, as a hoplite hurrying forward would more probably simply step over or around a fallen enemy and leave him to the light troops following up behind.

A more common, and more practical usage of the pointed butt-end would have been to stick it into the ground when the warrior had no immediate use for his spear. Not only was the 2.5kg weight (5.5lbs) burdensome when added to the rest of a hoplite's gear, but the weapon's length made it cumbersome to carry around, while the very sharp edge to the main spear-blade made the thing a hazard if left lying on the ground at ankle height. Impaling the spear into the ground with the blade above head height made a lot more sense.

In the phalanx the *doru*'s sharp butt-end must have been a definite hazard to those behind the hoplite. Some careful positioning was needed if the man at the front was not to stab the man behind as he drew back his spear for a thrust. Furthermore, the spear was usually held in the 'trail carry' position while the army was not in actual combat - that is the weapon was carried at knee height with an extended arm. Moving to the fighting position involved bringing the spear up so that it was held higher than the shield with the back end extending over the shoulder. Getting from position A to B required a lot of drill practice as this manoeuvre had to be performed in a tight formation of closely-packed men with an unwieldy length of wood that had a sharp point at each end.

Once in battle position, the spear was a formidable weapon. Modern tests have shown that the overhead stab was capable of driving the point clear through a human torso, shattering the ribs as it went by. The edge of the large stabbing blade could also give a vicious slash. Re-enactors have discovered a further advantage of using the *doru* rather than a sword. A sword involves several kilograms of steel held at the full extension of the arm. Even with considerable practice, using a sword in battle is a very tiring exercise that cannot be sustained for more than several minutes without the need for a rest.

The *doru* was held in a much more ergonomic position to start with, and the user could rest it against his shoulder without moving the spear from the 'ready' position. In other words, a hoplite in the phalanx could easily outlast a sword-wielding enemy. Also a slashing sword requires that the user needs at least five feet of battle line to avoid being a hazard to his own side, while the close-packed phalanx could put a man every three feet. So not only would three swordsman be fighting five hoplites, but they would tire faster.

This advantage of the *doru* explains why, once one Greek state had adopted the hoplite formation all the others had to do the same. This, despite the fact that the mountainous terrain of Greece was so unsuitable for hoplite warfare that battles had to be fought time and again on the few bits of flat land available (there have been six battles of Thermopylae to date), and the logistics of moving a hoplite army around were so complex that battles were sometimes scheduled in advance so that both sides knew where and when to turn up.

The Swords – *Kopis* and *Xiphos*

The *doru* was the weapon of choice in a phalanx battle line. However, outside the battle line the spear was little more than a cumbersome nuisance. In the ad hoc infantry skirmishes of informal warfare, a sword was invaluable. A swordsman did not need an organized squad formed about him to be effective, so a hoplite on patrol or sentry duty would have relied on his sword.

Those who believe that a sword is best swung lustily for maximum effect would have been fans of the *kopis*, which was basically a machete optimized for killing people. The heavy blade was widest towards the tip, and often had a slight crook to give extra impetus to a slash. Because the blade was one-edged, the pommel was asymmetrical, allowing it to be better modelled for a secure grip.

Both the *kopis* and the *xiphos* were made from a single piece of metal with the grips of the pommel fitted to a metal tang which extended to become the actual blade. The blade was around 60cm (2ft) long, though longer and shorter examples were readily available depending on the preference of the individual and his armourer.

The xiphos was double-edged and suited to a more practised style of fighting which allowed a thrust to go with the cut for which the *kopis* was optimized. The advantage of a stabbing blade is that it allowed a man to fight shoulder-to-shoulder with similarly-trained companions, and a thrust is harder to block than a slash. It comes as no surprise then that the Spartans seem to have preferred the *xiphos*.

Both swords were about the same weight (around 1kg or 2.5lbs), though the *xiphos* could be lighter as it could also be shorter and still effective. The apocryphal Spartan mother probably gave her son a *xiphos* when she was preparing him for combat. When the lad observed that the blade was somewhat on the short side, his mother laconically advised, 'stand closer'.

Armour

In his choice of armour, a hoplite had numerous options. Conformity in these matters is something of a modern European military obsession which was not shared by the Greeks. The main thing Greeks looked for in armour was that it did the best possible job of protecting the occupant. Because ancient blacksmithing was less than an exact science, the only way that a piece of armour could be trusted on the battlefield was for it to have been field tested on previous battlefields. Therefore sets of armour were treasured family possessions, handed from father to son, with the latest fashions being incorporated into the nation's stock as older pieces went missing in action or became unusable from being stressed beyond their design tolerance. Here we will examine a hoplite in his panoply, going from head to foot, examining each bit of his kit along the way.

The Helmet

The original archaic helmet was a sort of metal bucket with eye-holes. In the archaic era this slowly evolved to a design known – to modern researchers – as the Corinthian helmet. This was technically a helm, as it covered the full head and face. ('Helmet' is the diminutive of 'helm', as for example 'piglet' is the diminutive of 'pig'.) Usually beaten from a single piece of bronze or brass, the Corinthian was a distinctive item of armour that had the added advantage of making the wearer look formidably inhuman.

This effect was further enhanced by the large crest of horsehair or feathers atop the helmet which made the wearer look taller.

Many images of Spartan warriors show the crest as transverse – running from ear-to-ear rather than from forehead to neck as do other Greek crests. This may be typical Spartan contrariness, as some have postulated, or because the images discovered depict actual individuals. Since the kind of people who were likely to commission statuettes of themselves were wealthy, these were probably officers. So another theory is that the transverse crest indicated a Spartan officer. In rather the same way – and possibly not co-incidentally – it is very likely that the transverse crest later marked a Roman centurion.

The side parts of the helm were divided by a slit, so that when not in use the helm could be thrust up entirely and worn on the back of the head, with the flaps gripping the sides of the skull to hold it in place. This was how the helm was generally worn, since re-enactors report that being inside a Corinthian is a very warm and claustrophobic experience in which hearing is severely impaired. Nevertheless, since a hoplite in the battle line required only a focused field of vision and needed only to hear a few basic trumpet calls, the maximum protection it afforded made this helmet an enduring infantry favourite throughout our period.

Those who preferred to see and hear what was going on about them might prefer the 'Thracian' helmet. The Thracian focussed on its core competence of protecting the top and back of the skull, while the greater visibility it permitted gave the wearer responsibility for getting his face out of the way of trouble. However, the Thracian did have broad side flaps protecting the cheeks. The main advantage of the Thracian was that it could be worn continuously in position rather than being hurriedly thrust down over the head as the moment for battle arrived.

Anyone who envisaged spending combat time outside the ranks of the phalanx was probably better off in a Thracian helmet as this made – for example – skirmishing with a sword very much easier.

A compromise helmet which evolved around the early fifth century was the Chalcedean. This helmet type was based on the Corinthian but aimed at giving the wearer greater vision and hearing. The design was somewhat more complex than the basic Corinthian, but the extra effort would have been welcomed, especially by those such as unit commanders who needed to hear reports from subordinates and orders from higher ranks, even amid the din of battle when removing a helmet to hear better was ill-advised.

There were many other variations on these three main designs – in fact modern archaeologists identify almost twenty different types of helmet in use by fifth-century Greek armies. All gave considerable protection to the face. The exception was the cavalry helmet, sometimes called the 'Boeotian' helmet. This helmet appears to have been modelled on a standard horseman's hat, though the bronze downward-facing brim was designed to deflect arrows and sword strokes rather than raindrops. Nevertheless the brim did prevent the horseman from being blinded by the sun at a critical moment, and afforded the all-round visibility and free hearing essential to the cavalryman's function.

The Cuirass

As with the helmet, the discerning warrior was almost spoiled for choice in the selection of body armour available. The first issue to deal with when choosing this important item was the material. Bronze, linen or leather? Leather was a popular choice, though very different from the frankly homo-erotic designs of some modern film-makers (e.g. 300, Rise of an Empire). The name 'cuirass' in fact comes from the Latin for 'leather' (corium). Bull's hide was favoured for its thickness, and the leather was sometimes reinforced with metal plates giving extra protection to the chest.

The older choice was bronze. This type of armour was slightly flared at the waist to allow the wearer to bend, and this flare has given the design its modern name of the 'bell cuirass'. As ever with body armour, every item was a compromise between lightness and protection. We know exactly the weight of one bell cuirass – 3.36kg (7.4 lbs). This is the 'Argos cuirass' which was discovered almost intact. (Described in detail in Schwartz, A. 'Reinstating the Hoplite: Arms, Armour and Phalanx Fighting in Archaic and Classical Greece'. Historia Einzelschriften 207. Stuttgart: Franz Steiner Verlag, 2009)

Modern reconstructions put the Argos cuirass on the light

side, and suggest that a more common weight range was between 4-10kg depending on the wearer's strength and sense of vulnerability. (cf p147ff of *Reconstructing Ancient Linen Body Armor: Unraveling the Linothorax Mystery* Aldrete G, Scott Bartell, S, and Alicia Aldrete, A Johns Hopkins University Press 2009).

One advantage that the leather and bronze types of cuirass gave was that they made the wearer look absolutely splendid. As Socrates once pointed out to an armourer, it was possible to get 'form-fitting' armour that nevertheless made an ugly body look like an Apollo. Not for nothing are some of these designs known as the 'muscle cuirass'. Armourers carefully sculpted the armour to make the wearer appear to have a narrow waist with magnificently wide muscular shoulders and intimidating pectorals. This was important to the average Greek warrior, who prepared for battle as carefully as a modern teenage girl for a party. It would never do for a warrior to go into battle looking anything less than his best.

Therefore the most practical armour of the lot was definitely not in the spirit of the thing. This was the linothorax. The linothorax was made not out of the traditional materials, but linen. The Greeks had discovered that multiple layers of linen stiffened and glued together made tough but flexible armour. Vase paintings show that the separate flaps which go over the shoulder of linothorax armour were straight until bent into shape when they were strapped down.

Arrow tests have shown that this linen armour was about one sixth as effective as the same thickness of bronze but twelve times lighter. In other words, one can get about the same protection from linen armour as from bronze at about half the weight. This reduction would have been less because most hoplites opted for extra protection in the form of scale armour around the midriff or extra metal plates protecting heart and lungs. Nevertheless, the full panoply including weapons weighed between 19-30kg (41-60lbs) depending on the wearer's individual choices, so something that could knock 4kg from this load would have been worth serious consideration.

Vases showing warriors preparing for battle suggest that the linothorax was donned rather like some modern girdles, being wrapped around the waist and then secured with laces. Shoulder flaps were then strapped down afterwards to complete the set. The cuirass was designed with a front and back section. The two halves were united around the wearer's body by straps in the case of leather and with eyebolts and pins in the case of bronze.

All varieties of body armour came with a set of *pteruges* ('feathers'). These 'feathers' were actually lengths of thick leather (or for linothorax enthusiasts, linen and resin strips). They were arranged to hang from the waist to just above the knee with each edge slightly overlapping. The result was that the wearer had a thick protective skirt when he was standing still, but almost complete freedom of movement when his lower body was in motion.

Greaves

Finally, the lower part of the leg might be encased in greaves. Greaves were a sort of footless metal sock that came to just below the knee. Preferably made from brass, some greaves clamped onto the leg once the springy sides had been opened from the back. Other designs used straps and buckles. All had some form of felt padding within as their main purpose was to protect the bones below the knee which lie just under the skin and are vulnerable to impact.

Greaves, like almost all other parts of the panoply apart from shield, spear and helmet, were optional. They were most popular among hoplites fighting irregular troops who used missile weapons such as arrows or javelins. Once the battle lines met, most of a warrior's lower extremities were safe from the *doru*, but in the preliminaries a hoplite in the front ranks might certainly appreciate protection for his vulnerable shins.

There are depictions of warriors choosing to wear only a single greave on the advanced leg. While this saves on weight and expense, re-enactors report that it takes considerable practice to be able to march comfortably with such an arrangement.

Overall

The hoplite panoply was a highly efficient combination of offensive power and defensive durability. The design was optimized for a warrior fighting in a phalanx with his comrades, but it was flexible enough to allow the wearer considerable freedom of movement in less formal combat situations. Hoplites could, and did, sprint in full battle gear. In fact running while in full armour was one of the premier events at the Olympic Games.

In modern terms, a panoply cost about the equivalent of a family car – somewhere between six months to a year's wages for a workman. As with the automobile, there was considerable variance in this figure, depending if the purchaser wanted a battered but serviceable second-hand version for his teenage son or to impress his peers with a state-of-the-art model with all the latest technology. Given the expense involved, it is unremarkable that, rather than pursue a beaten enemy for any distance, a victorious Greek army busied itself in stripping the valuable spoils of war from the bodies of the deceased. It was traditional to hand back the corpses of the slain to the families of the losers. The armour stayed with the victors. (In later years the Athenian state would subsidize a new panoply for the sons of a warrior who had fallen in battle and could not pass down the family armour to the next generation.)

One of the factors which made Sparta such a formidable force on the battlefield was that thanks to the *kleros* system of land distribution, every Spartiate could afford a full panoply of armour. (In later centuries this system became a drawback as land was concentrated in the hands of a few and the number of Spartiates dropped precipitously.)

However, at this time Lacedaemonia supported around 7,000 of the finest heavy infantrymen in the known world. This was not only because the Spartans were well-equipped, but because they, of all Greek nations, most fully realized that the full potential of the phalanx formation could only be achieved through relentless drill. The hoplites of the phalanx worked best not as individuals but as components of a larger organism, and it is to this that we now turn.

Unit Formation

Other Greeks went into battle in *taxis*, but the Spartans marched in a *lochos*. Each was a formation of 500-1500 men which made up the basic component of a phalanx. The Spartan *lochos* was formed from a smaller formation called a *pentekostyes*. It is probable that each of the original villages from which Sparta was formed each formed their own *lochos*, the combined *lochoi* comprising the Spartan phalanx. (In later years the *lochos* was reorganized into a smaller unit.)

A complete description of how the Spartan army formed up for battle does not exist for this period. It is clear that later events – namely the Peloponnesian War and its aftermath – forced considerable changes upon the Spartan army, and the descriptions we have of unit formations date to after those changes. Thucydides was the first historian to make a serious attempt to discover exactly how the Spartan army was organized. He was largely unsuccessful, because the Spartans were a generally secretive people in the first place, and in the second place, Sparta was at that time at war with Athens and Thucydides was an Athenian general (albeit retired).

Therefore a full description of Spartan battle formations must await the text of Xenophon. Also a former general, Xenophon has a military man's eye and passion for detail, but his description comes from over a century later in a period when military tactics were fast evolving. Therefore we must for the present be content with only a rough outline of the Spartan army formation of the late sixth century.

While all Spartiates were theoretically equal, on the battlefield the army was highly hierarchical with almost every man slotted into a carefully designed command structure. While the phalanx is often described as a 'battle-line', the basic unit, the *enomotia*, did not form in ranks – sideways along the line – but in files – lines of men which formed up behind the man facing the enemy. The warriors of *enomotia* were literally 'sworn men', though it is not clear what they swore or to whom. According to Herodotus (1.65) the group of thirty-nine men consisted as nearly as possible of one member of each service year class. That is, with one man aged 20, the next aged 21, and so on up to the retirement age of a Spartan warrior, which was 59.

This unit could form up eight men deep, which was the usual formation, or be split into smaller files standing side-by-side, depending on the length of the battle line required by the *strategos* (general). The position of honour was the front rank, with the rest of the unit sandwiched between this man and his second who took the rearmost rank. Each *enomotia* was doubled up to form a further unit which was called a 'fifty' (*pentekostyes*).

A bit of basic arithmetic will show that the numbers in two *enomotia* and a *pentekostyes* do not match, but unit numbers were flexible. (Rather as a Roman 'century' actually contained about eighty men.) As a result there has been considerable discussion as to the exact nature of the early *pentekostyes*. For example Thucydides (5.68.3) says that there were two *pentekostyes* in the next unit size up – the *lochos*. However, Xenophon reckons the Spartans came in at four *pentekostyes* to the *lochos*. Just to complicate things further, both Xenophon and Thucydides reckon that the *lochos* was itself a sub-unit of a larger unit called the *mora*. However in the late sixth century and early fifth the *mora* does not seem to exist, and the *lochos* is the largest unit of the army.

There has been considerable discussion in learned journals on this topic, and little consensus. For instance Lazenby (Lazenby J. *The Spartan Army* Stackpole Books 1985 p.9ff) and Connolly (Connolly P, *Greece and Rome at War* Macdonald 1981, p.41) offer irreconcilable versions of what Spartan formations looked like.

It is however abundantly clear that the early fifth century Spartan army had a clear rank structure (though we cannot know now what it was with any certainty) and each unit had both a commander and a second-in-command who could take over in the event of anything terminal happening to the original leader.

The late sixth century army was led by a King, though recent developments had resulted in only one King being present at a time. The King had a 'bodyguard' of 300 '*hippeis*'. Despite their title – which means 'cavalry' - these bodyguards were neither horsemen nor charged particularly with protecting the royal person. The title seems to have been both honorary and an honour for which Spartans competed fiercely. In battle the *hippeis* claimed the 'place of honour', though this might mean foremost in the battle-line, or on the very right of it. It was also typical of the Spartan mentality that a Spartan who competed to join the *hippeis* and failed was supposed to rejoice in the fact that, excellent fellow as he knew himself to be, his city had 300 men who were still better.

The place of honour was by implication one of the least safe places on the battlefield, so it comes as no surprise that members of this elite unit had to be replaced annually, with special officials called *hippagretai* to select from among the candidates. To qualify for consideration a candidate had to be married with at least one son so that the family line would continue even if the man selected fell in battle. The number 300 is immediately recognizable as the size of the force which was later to hold the line at Thermopylae. It is therefore very probable that those who fought and died in this battle were indeed the king and his *hippeis*.

If we know little about the actual organization of the Spartans themselves, we know even less about the *perioiki* who were obliged to fight alongside the Spartiates in battle. It is very probable that the *perioiki* used tactical formations similar to those of the Spartiates themselves, and they certainly formed up to the left of the Spartans when the phalanx was drawn up.

The allies of the Peloponnesian League were obliged no less than the *perioiki* to be present and fight alongside the Spartans. These allies undoubtedly adopted their own individual battle formations, and it is also probable that some of the less wealthy Arcadian tribes provided the Spartan army with its skirmishers and light missile troops.

The Spartans had little time for cavalry, and indeed cavalry seem to have had only a peripheral role on contemporary battlefields. The main functions of cavalry lay in reconnaissance, and in covering the retreat of a broken unit. Cavalry are at their best among men in broken formation, so the presence of enemy horsemen made it harder to follow up against fleeing infantry because of the dangers inherent in a unit losing formation.

When faced by the shield wall of a phalanx, cavalry were useless in a direct assault, and since the Spartans believed that a direct assault was all that their army needed for victory, this alone explains why cavalry were not deemed particularly important. It is worth noting however that it is probable that the early cavalry formation was a *mora*, and it was from this usage that formations of the same size and name came to be adopted by the later army.

Finally we come to the helots. The Spartan obsession with the threat of a helot rebellion and the necessity of keeping the helots under control at all times made the Spartans reluctant to venture very far from home in case the army had to turn back to deal with a revolt.

One solution to the problem was for the army to take the helots with them. This idea is supported by an unambiguous statement from Herodotus who tells us that this was what the Spartans actually did. In Book IX of his *History* he tells us repeatedly that the Spartans had a large helot component to their army (Herodotus *History* 9.10.1, 9.28.2, 9.29.1). The question was what the helots were doing there, because Herodotus nowhere tells us this. Some (e.g. Hunt, P. 'Helots at the Battle of Plataea' *Historia*: 2nd Qtr. 1997, pp. 129-144) have argued that the helots actually were armed and fought in battle alongside their Spartan masters.

This contention seems improbable simply because of the vast number of helots involved. At the Battle of Plataea in 479 we are told that there were seven helots for every Spartan. From an estimate of the Spartan numbers, we get 35,000 helots. From a Spartan perspective this is an alarming number of potential enemies to have under arms and trained in warfare. Given that the number of Spartiates at this time was no more than 6,000 to 8,000, these men would give the Spartans a run for their money in a Spartan-helot battle, let alone if the helots decided to turn on the Spartans in mid-battle while the army was fighting someone else.

We do know that in later years the Spartans definitely did have helots under arms, because 700 helot hoplites accompanied the general Brasidas to Thrace in the Peloponnesian War of the late fifth century. However, Brasidas made sure that these helots were only a minor component of his overall force, and that he took them far away.

While we have to accept the figures given by Herodotus that there was a large helot contingent with a Spartan army, an alternative hypothesis would be that only a small minority – if that – actually bore arms. The others would have served as retainers and camp followers. The Spartans even in peacetime were not very good at doing for themselves, and in war they would have seen no reason to manage without cooks, blacksmiths and personal attendants. Furthermore, we need not be sure that all these helots were even adult males. The reason for so many helots being present might be because women and minors could do most of the scut-work around camp, and they also served as very useful hostages should the helot menfolk get any ideas about rebelling while the Spartan army was away.

Chapter Ten

The Road to Marathon

The suppression of the Ionian Rebellion of 499 to 493 had left the Greek cities of Asia Minor firmly under the control of the Persian Empire. Far from incidentally, that same revolt had also drawn the attention of the Persians rulers to the Greek mainland from whence so much support from the rebels had come. This was unfortunate, as the Persians were currently in search of new worlds to conquer.

At this time the Achaemenid Persian Empire (as it is properly known) was near its peak, stretching from central Asia to the shores of the Mediterranean. However, to the north of the empire there was now nowhere for the Persians to expand but the barren Ural steppes and the even more barren lands to the east of that. To the south lay the ocean and in the east the empire now butted against the mountain massif of the Himalayas.

Egypt had already fallen, so in terms of further conquests for Persia's expansionist leaders there remained two interesting projects. The conquest of India, and the conquest of Europe – starting with Greece. India was prosperous, populous and well-armed. Greece looked the easier proposition. It was – from a Persian perspective – small and relatively primitive. Even better, it was divided into numerous city-states which could be conquered piecemeal. Already ambassadors had been sent out to demand submission to the King of Kings. For every ambassador who had received the Spartan treatment (it will be recalled that in Sparta the Persian ambassador was thrown down a well), others had been treated with courtesy, or even welcome.

For some Greek cities the existential threat to Hellenistic independence meant less than the opportunity to use Persian power to get one up on a hated neighbour. Thus, for example, once Sparta had emphatically rejected the Persian overtures, Argos immediately became pro-Persian and was to remain adamantly neutral even as Persian armies advanced into the Greek mainland. As we have seen the people of the island of

Aegina submitted readily to Persian overtures, infuriating the Athenians and bringing the Spartans, led by Cleomenes, to the island.

This mixed reception gave the Persians hope that rather than face a united Greece, they could complete their next phase of imperial expansion step-by-step, taking down individual states as the opportunity presented itself. There could be no doubt as to which city was top of the Persian hit list. Athens had not only supported the Ionian revolt, it had put itself forward as the rebellion's leader. Currently a state of open war existed between Athens and Persia, and it was only a matter of time before doing something drastic about Athens reached the top of the Persian agenda.

In fact the invasion of Greece had commenced immediately after the end of the Ionian Rebellion. This had not been properly noted by the Greeks themselves, because the initial Persian advance had been through Thrace to Macedonia, and there was considerable debate among the classical Greeks as to whether the Macedonians were properly Greeks at all. Certainly, to the Spartans comfortably dug into the mountains on the other side of Hellas, the Persian threat remained almost as far away as ever. Nevertheless, this northern phase of the invasion was accomplished with the smooth precision of long practice, and was an ominous harbinger for the future. The general in charge of the northern invasion was one Mardonius. Mardonius was son-in-law to the King of Kings, Darius himself, which is a sign of how seriously the Persians were taking their intended conquest.

The invasion of Greece. Attempt Number One

Mardonius' campaigns of 492 left Persia's armies on the border with Macedon. Macedon had given token submission to the Persian Empire for over a century, but now with the harsh reality of a Persian army on hand, that submission became real and Macedon was forced into Persian vassalage.

With the north secure, the Persians moved on to the question of how to get at Greece proper. As the Romans were to discover three centuries later when attempting to invade Macedonia from the other direction, it is not that easy for an army to get between Macedonia and Thessaly. The Olympos Range lies between the two regions, and the many peaks of this range include Mount Olympus itself, almost 3km (9,800 feet) high and the only outstanding feature of a generally rugged landscape. Getting an army through the narrow passes was a tactical and logistical nightmare in itself, let alone if those passes were blocked by heavily armoured Greek hoplites whose phalanx formation could almost have been designed for the job.

Unsurprisingly, the Persians decided to bypass the mountains and take their army south by sea. Herodotus takes up the story:

'Mardonius now advanced through Europe toward Eretria and Athens.

That is, these two cities were the excuse for the expedition, but the true intention was to conquer as many Greek cities as possible along the way. The people of Thasos found this out the hard way, because though they had done nothing against the King, the island was nevertheless taken by the naval force. Meanwhile the Macedonians were conscripted into the land army just as the tribes to the east had already been.

From Thasos the naval contingent crossed to the mainland and sailed along the coast to Acanthus. From here the fleet attempted to round Mount Athos [while carrying the army].'

Herodotus *History* 6.46

At this point it is necessary to enlarge on the geography with which Herodotus' Greek audience was intimately familiar. Thasos is an island in the north Aegean Sea close to the coast of the modern Greek province of East Macedonia. Just to the west lies the three-fingered peninsula of the Chalcidice which has the modern city of Thessalonica at the base of the north-western part. Diagonally across from Thessalonica, on the south-eastern side is Mount Athos, a peninsula around 10km (7 miles) wide and stretching 50km (30 miles) southward into the Aegean Sea.

It was still fairly early in the campaigning season, and the Persians were in a hurry to get south. Therefore they paid less heed to the weather than the more sea-savvy Greeks would have done. Years of navigating the treacherous seas of this coast had taught the Greeks that at this time of year one should exercise caution when putting to sea with a fishing boat, let alone with an entire fleet of transports. Almost inevitably …

> 'The wind came up – a violent northerly which pushed aside everything in its path. It gave the fleet some very turbulent treatment, sinking many and shattering a large number on the rocks of Athos. Reports put the number of ships destroyed at just under 300, and the human toll at over 20,000. [This assumes a reasonable contingent of around seventy passengers and crew on each ship.] The sea around Athos is fuller of monsters than anywhere else, and these animals seized and devoured one group of victims. Another group, those who could not swim, were drowned, and those who could were smashed against the rocks when they reached land. Others died of exposure from the cold.'
>
> (ibid.)

News of this disaster spread quickly, and the tribes of Thrace decided that the depletion of the Persian army at the hands of Neptune gave them the opportunity to retaliate for the rough handling they had received at the hands of Mardonius. A tribe called the Brygi launched a night attack on the Persian camp where the remnant of the army was based. This attack was unexpected and correspondingly successful. Many Persians were killed and Mardonius himself was wounded.

Since he now lacked both the men and the ships to proceed with the invasion of southern Greece, Mardonius dedicated himself to vindictively hunting down and vanquishing the Brygi. In this he was successful, but the addition of a handful of Thracian tribes to the Persian empire was hardly the objective for which so much money and materiel had been gathered, even when the conquest of Thasos was added to the tally. The expedition had failed, and Mardonius was recalled in disgrace.

The conquest of Greece. Attempt Number Two

The Greeks might have breathed easy at this evidence that Hellas was protected by its gods, but they still had cause to fear the dogged perseverance of the Persians. In fact, almost as soon as he received the news of the loss of the fleet at Athos, King

Darius had sent orders for his vassal states on the Mediterranean seaboard to prepare new ships. (The new fleet included the ships of the hapless Thasians, for they had mustered a small but tidy fleet to defend their island. This the numerically superior Persians had simply confiscated.)

The disgraced Mardonius was told to sit out this next attempt, which was to be commanded by a Persian general called Datis and a colleague called Artaphernes who was one of King Darius' nephews. Brainstorming sessions during the preparatory phases had come up with a new plan. Rather than painfully work their way down from the north, this time the Persians would boldly strike across the sea toward Athens. Admittedly this involved spending more time on the water than anyone would like, but it also meant the Persians could stay away from the Athos promontory, which they had come to dread.

The new invasion fleet was huge, numbering over 600 ships, both war triremes and transports for men and cavalry. When this armada reached its first destination, the island of Naxos, the overawed population made no attempt to defend their city but instead fled *en masse* to the hills. For the Persians it was an encouraging start. They burned the city and enslaved whatever inhabitants they could flush out of the mountain caves, and moved on to their next target.

Island-hopping in this way, the Persians moved inexorably toward Eretria and Athens beyond that. The people of the island of Delos fled the Persian advance, even though the Persians demonstrated that same religious sensitivity that they showed elsewhere in their empire, and promised that neither the population nor shrines of the sacred island of Apollo and Artemis would be harmed.

And so to Eretria, on the large island of Euboea, from where the fields of Attica were visible on a clear day. The people of Eretria greeted the imminent arrival of the Persians with a mixture of panic and disarray. Some were for following the Naxian example and abandoning the city, while others were prepared to fight to the death to defend their homeland. Still others were for promptly surrendering once that the Persian force was upon them, in the hope that prompt and total submission would spare them the worst of the Persians' wrath.

The Athenians had responded to an earlier call for help from the Eretrians, and had sent a force of 4,000 hoplites to help with the defence of the city. However, once the Athenians arrived and saw for themselves the chaos and confusion among the inhabitants they concluded that the lack of unity among the Eretrians made the city indefensible. Accordingly they sailed home again, and arrived shortly before the news that, as predicted, Eretria had fallen and its people had been enslaved or put to the sword. It was a grim warning to the Athenians of what to expect, since no-one was in any doubt about where the Persians were going next.

In fact, the Persians went to Marathon, twenty miles to the north-east of Athens. Here the broad coastal plain was thickly overgrown with the fennel which gave the place its name. (Fennel, a sweet savoury herb is a staple of Mediterranean cookery, and is called 'Marathon' in Greek.) This open terrain was ideal for manoeuvre by cavalry, in which arm of warfare the Persians were vastly superior.

Unlike the Eretrians, the Athenians were pretty clear on how they intended to proceed. The city would fight. To this end every able-bodied citizen was called to arms, and since the entire Athenian force was outnumbered around twelve to one, the Athenians sent urgently to the rest of Greece for reinforcements. From the Athenian perspective it was clear that the Persians had not come for the Athenians alone, but to conquer the whole of Greece. Therefore it was logical that, out of sheer self-preservation, the whole of Greece should come to the defence of Athens, however much animosity individual city-states might feel for the Athenians themselves.

In reality, and rather as the Persians had calculated, no such thing happened. The cities of Greece understood the logic. They also understood that if they came and stood with the Athenians and no-one else did, then by supporting Athens they would have just bumped themselves into prime position as the next target on the Persian hit list. Therefore either all the Greeks had to respond unanimously or no-one at all was going to come to the aid of the Athenians. Given the highly individualistic and fractious nature of the Greek city-states, only a deranged optimist would have expected them all suddenly to pull together – even in the face of an existential threat such as the Persians posed.

There was one city which immediately mustered an army to join the Athenian force, and that was a contingent from tiny Plataea, which sent the entire 1,000 men that the city was capable of mustering. There were two reasons for this. The first was that Plataea was not that far from Athens, and there was a risk that the Persians might gulp down the city as an incidental bonus of conquest, rather as the Thasians had been taken by the Persian army while it was en route to Macedonia. Secondly, and more altruistically, the Athenians had been good to the Plataeans, and it was time to return the favour.

Several years previously, an expansionist Thebes had been pressing Plataea to join the city in a Boeotian confederation. Plataea had refused. Because Sparta was seen as the foremost military power and also the city with the greatest moral rectitude in Greece, the Plataeans turned to Sparta for help. The Spartans declined, and suggested that the Athenians might make better protectors. This was logical enough because Athens and Sparta were on relatively good terms at the time, and Athens was much nearer. Herodotus was not the only Greek who cynically suspected that the Spartan suggestion was actually maliciously intended to poison relationships between Athens and Thebes.

If this was the intention, it certainly succeeded. To preserve Plataean independence, Athens had ended up fighting a brisk little war with the Boeotians. The Athenians won, the river Asopus was fixed as the border between Thebes and Plataea, and the Plataeans were eternally grateful.

While welcome, 1,000 Plataeans had not much more than symbolic value. What Athens really needed was the Spartans. If Sparta hurried to the aid of Athens, then such was the hold that Sparta had on the Greek psyche that other Greek states would seriously consider joining the fray – not least because if the Spartan-Athenian alliance carried the day, they might later ask pointed questions of any abstainers.

Consequently a messenger was dispatched post-haste to call the Spartans to arms. That messenger was a runner called Pheidippides. It is a little-known fact that over a long distance, a well-trained human can out-pace a horse, especially if that distance includes broken and mountainous terrain. Therefore all

Greek states maintained messengers trained to cover substantial distances in a remarkably short time.

In this case Pheidippides faced a 246km (153 mile) jog to Sparta while taking in the occasional mountain range in the process. According to Herodotus, Pheidippides set off the moment the news came that Eretria had fallen. He did the run in a day and a half. (This was recently verified as possible by modern runners who have proven that the run can be done in just over a day provided that the runner is extremely fit and prepared to be prostrated by exhaustion afterwards. Pheidippides took longer on his trip because he had to run home again with the Spartan reply.)

The Spartans might not have particularly welcomed the arrival of the heroic runner. From a reference by the philosopher Plato it seems that the helots of Messenia were getting restless. This might have been expected. That the enemy of one's enemy was a friend was a concept as well known in antiquity as it is today, so now that the Persians were actually in Greece, the helots might have viewed them as potential allies and liberators. Supporting the idea of helot unrest, we also get a reference in Strabo to a Messenian War, otherwise unknown, which must have happened around this point, and our old friend Pausanias mentions Messenians fleeing to Sicily in the early fifth century after an unsuccessful revolt. So it would appear that the Spartans might have wanted to keep at least some of their army at home to keep an eye on their restive subject population.

Furthermore, from the Spartan perspective, the Athenians had asked for trouble. They had voluntarily involved themselves in the Ionian revolt, an event the cautious Spartans had chosen to sit out. Therefore the Spartans might argue that the Athenians had not consulted them before sailing to Asia Minor (where they had marched on the Persian provincial capital of Sardis and burned it to the ground). Given this sort of behaviour, it was not unreasonable for the Persians to decide to pay a reciprocal visit to Athens, bringing firewood with them. It was however unreasonable for the Athenians to ask the Spartans to bail them out of the trouble caused largely by their own recklessness.

Nevertheless, much as they might have wished to do so, the Spartans could not simply tell the Athenians to go hang. For a start, and whatever the provocation that had brought them there, the Persians were in Greece, and their invasion was unlikely to stop at Athens. If it looked inevitable that the Spartans were going to have to fight the Persians to defend their own independence, then fighting that war a good distance from Laconia might be a good idea.

Secondly, the whole of Hellas looked to the Spartans for leadership. The Spartans knew that their resources and manpower were stretched in this role, but it would be fatal for the rest of Greece to discover that. Therefore Sparta had either to lead, or accept that the Greeks would look for other leaders.

Ideally, what would suit the Spartans best was for the Athenians to fight the Persians to a standstill on their own, and for both sides to get severely mauled in the fracas. Then the Spartans could bring up their army, take on the Persians while they were licking their wounds, and hopefully defeat them. Thereafter the Spartans would appear as the liberators of Greece, and their Athenian rivals (to a Greek city-state any other city-state was a rival) would have been brutally crippled.

This crippling would happen even in the unlikely event of an Athenian victory, for it was hard to imagine the Athenians overcoming such odds without taking massive casualties. If the Athenians won, the Spartans would still come out on top, because they would now have an intact army – and the most feared army in Greece at that – positioned in front of a near-defenceless Athens. This would be a perfect time for the Spartans to discuss with the Athenians the matter of changing their radical democratic government for a proper oligarchy. The Spartans disliked and distrusted democracy, which they equated with mob rule, and had made sure that none of it cropped up in the Peloponnesian League.

In short it was hard to see how letting the Persians and Athenians fight it out could go wrong for Sparta. All the Spartans needed was an excuse for turning up slightly late for the event. And as it happened they had such an excuse readily to hand.

The Karneia was an ancient Dorian festival. It was sacred to the God Apollo, though even the ancients were confused as to the origins of the event. As far as is known, the celebration was to do with the return of the Heraclidae (p.14), and this had merged with an even older harvest ritual. The date of this festival is controversial, and important as it is the main means by which the Battle of Marathon is dated, and therefore the date of this battle is likewise uncertain. The problem is that calendars in the Greek world were flexible. They had to be, because the lunar month was the basis of all Greek calendars, and the lunar month does not fit at all tidily into the solar year.

From various descriptions, it appears that the Karneia might kick off on any day between 15 August and 17 September, in rather the same way that the modern celebration of Easter might vary by almost a month depending on the circumstances. The most important thing about the Karneia was that, on the final night of the celebration on the ninth day, the full moon should remain in the sky all night.

Pheidippides arrived with his fateful message on the third day, when the Karneia had almost a week to run. If we are to accept the brutal *Realpolitik* which suggests that a Spartan delay might be expedient, then from a Laconian viewpoint, the timing was near-perfect. The Spartans could justifiably argue that they could do nothing for a week while the festival was progressing to its climax. Then they could set out for Athens, speeding up or delaying their journey so as to arrive just after the inevitable Persian-Athenian clash, and thereafter save the day (though sadly, not the Athenian army). Nor could the rest of the Greeks blame the Spartans for their tardy arrival, since everyone knew that the Spartans were devoutly religious and obedient to their gods.

Accordingly, the messenger was sent back to Athens with the message that Sparta was totally behind the Athenian effort to repel the foreign invader. The Spartan army would be on the way as soon as possible once the Spartan religious celebrations had been wrapped up. Until then the Athenians were on their own.

The Battle of Marathon

There were a number of Greeks in the Persian army at Marathon. These included the deposed tyrant Hippias (pp. 101-103), whom the Persians intended to re-instate as the puppet ruler of the city once the Athenians had been conquered. As the former, and potential future ruler of Athens, Hippias had a good number of friends, including those openly supporting his cause in the Persian army, and clandestine supporters among the Athenian forces. Because of these secret supporters, Hippias and the Persians probably knew the Spartan reply almost as soon as the Athenians did.

The Persian and Athenian armies that faced each other across the plain of Marathon were currently at something of a stalemate. The Persians wanted the Athenians to advance on to the plain, where they could be perforated by the massed ranks of Persian bowmen, and ridden down by Persian cavalry. The Athenians wanted the Persians to remain bottled up on the plain while they awaited their Spartan reinforcements. As a result the Athenian army occupied the low hills surrounding Marathon, and challenged the Persian army to force its way out.

This the Persians were reluctant to do. Though they vastly outnumbered the Athenians, modern research suggests that the bulk of their army was untrained levies and oarsmen for the fleet. In terms of trained regular troops, Persia probably had some 30,000 men plus around another 1,000 cavalry. The cavalry and levies would be of little use attacking a well-entrenched phalanx, so if it came to forcing the passes between the hills, the Persian numerical superiority dropped to 3-1 – not particularly good odds for troops intending to force a well-defended position.

Nevertheless, the impending arrival of the Spartans meant that the Persians had to do something. Accordingly, it appears that they decided to split their army. One large force would remain on the plain, holding the Athenians in check, while another large force would embark on the ships and attempt an end-run around the Athenian army by sailing to invade the city of Athens itself. If the Athenian army split to match the Persian deployment, its numbers would be too few to hold the passes. If the whole army hurried back to Athens it would fight on less favourable ground, exhausted after a 20-mile forced march. Consequently, the threat of the Persian deployment forced the Athenians to do exactly what the Persians wanted. The Athenian army advanced on to the plain of Marathon to do battle.

The battle itself has been the topic of much scholarly discussion. We need not concern ourselves overly with this, as our focus is on Sparta, and the Spartans were not present at the battle. However, this was the first clash of Hellenes and Persians on mainland Greece, so the highlights are worth recording.

As mentioned earlier, the main strength of the Persians lay in their cavalry and archers. Cavalry are little use against formed infantry, because even the most unintelligent horse will not throw itself on a wall of men bristling with spears. Also, because ancient cavalry did not have stirrups, it was hard for a rider to brace himself in the saddle against a major shock. (Which is why the couched lance did not become popular until the Middle Ages.) Therefore the Persians intended to wear down the advancing Greeks with bow fire until they became demoralized and their formation became ragged. Then the Persian infantry would charge, and the cavalry hit the Athenian army on the flanks. It was a technique perfected in the Ionian rebellion, and it worked.

The Athenians knew it worked, because they too had participated in the Ionian rebellion. However, they had no intention of letting the Persians follow their winning formula in Attica. So as the Persians let fly their first volley of arrows, the entire Athenian army charged the Persians at a full sprint. This was the first time anyone had tried this, and it took the Persians completely by surprise. The first volley of arrows sailed over the heads of the charging Athenians and landed on the empty sand where they had been. There was not time to do much reloading, because soon afterwards the Athenians were on to the Persian lines.

A fully-armoured hoplite against a Persian bowman meant that superiority in armour and familiarity with hand-to-hand fighting made up for much of the Athenians' numerical inferiority. A cunning deployment by the Athenian general more than compensated for the rest. Herodotus (*History* 113ff) takes up the tale.

'The barbarians [i.e. the Persians and their subjects] were winning in the centre of the battle line, for here the Persians themselves were stationed. They broke the ranks of their attackers and began to pursue them inland.'

What the Persians did not realise was that the centre had been made weak by design.

> 'On both wings the Athenians and the Plataeans were winning. On routing those before them, they let the defeated enemy flee unhindered. Instead the two wings pivoted and attacked those who had broken the centre of their line.'
>
> (ibid.)

In short the Persian centre, which contained their army's best troops, had run into a trap. By surging forward after their initial success, they had allowed the enemy hoplites to envelop their flanks. It was a manoeuvre which the Carthaginian general Hannibal was to use in much the same way at Cannae over two centuries later, and with the same devastating success. The army, attacked on three sides panicked, failed to maintain formation, and was massacred.

> 'The Athenians were victorious. They followed up against the fleeing Persians and cut them down as they fled. When they reached the beach they tried to capture some ships and burn others.'
>
> (ibid.)

Perhaps because they had already started embarking (by some theories the cavalry horses had already boarded, which explains their absence from accounts of the battle), the Persians were able to put to sea and escape with a good remnant of their army. They had taken thousands of casualties, but their fleet was intact. Therefore this seemed a good moment to try Plan B, and see if anything could be achieved by sailing around Attica to Athens and seeing if the city could be taken while the army was away.

Aware of the risk, the Athenians sent a runner to both announce the victory and to warn the reserves to man the walls. By later accounts this runner was the indefatigable Pheidippides, who passed away once he had announced the news. However, near contemporary accounts give a number of different names for this runner. It was only centuries later that it was reported to be the same man who went to Sparta and back and then completed the run to Athens to announce the victory. This latter run, from the battlefield to Athens, has become immortalized as the standard distance of a long-distance run – the Marathon.

When the Persians found the Athenian reserves manning the city walls they realized that the city would not fall to a surprise attack. Therefore their general pulled his army back while he digested the extraordinary events of the day. One little city had taken on the power of the entire Persian Empire – and won.

When the Spartans arrived the next day, they found a rather tired but intact Athenian army. According to Herodotus, 192 Athenians and eleven Plataeans had died, while the Persians had been slaughtered in their thousands. It was a famous victory – easily the greatest Greek victory since the capture of Troy. The Athenians had single-handedly thrown back the Persian invader (the Plataeans tended to get edited out of later accounts) and saved European civilization.

All that anyone would later remember of the Spartans is that they had been too tardy to arrive in time for the battle, and the greatest victory on Greek soil had been won without them. It was a spectacular success for Athens and a humiliating setback for Sparta's military reputation. Even as the Persians abandoned their invasion and fell back in disorder, the Spartans knew that they would have to do something very special to make up for their non-performance at Marathon.

So they did.

Chapter Eleven

Thermopylae: Their Finest Hour

Invasion Postponed

Invasion attempt number three took much longer to launch against Greece than the Persians had intended. This was at least partly due to an unexpected side effect of the battle of Marathon. At Marathon a relatively small Athenian (and Plataean) army had trounced the much larger Persian force. This got people in other parts of the Persian Empire thinking. If Persia was not so invincible after all, perhaps it was possible for states with much larger armies than Athens to also throw off Persian rule, and resume the independence they had enjoyed before assimilation by the empire.

It took time for news of the Persian defeat to percolate around Persian dominions, because the Persians were not exactly keen on advertising it. Even when the news had reached the right ears, there was still the matter of properly getting organized for a full-scale rebellion. Thus though Marathon was fought in 490 BC, it took four years for the Egyptians to rebel, though there are also reports that the eastern frontier of the Persian empire had been in turmoil for much longer.

Unfortunately for the Egyptian rebels, four years was also what it took the Persians to rebuild and re-organize their army after the debacle at Marathon. (This rebuilding also involved a rise in taxes which helped to spur secessionist sentiment in rebellious states.) The coincidence of the rebel and Persian time-scales meant that the Egyptians rebelled just as the Persians had managed to get a large army operational once more. This worked out well for the Greeks, because the Persian army gathered for the third invasion of Greece had instead to be deployed to crush the Egyptians.

The strain of dealing with the Egyptian rebellion finally put paid to the ageing king Darius. This led to further delays in the Persian military build-up against Greece while the inevitable succession crisis played out. Eventually a man called Khashayarsha ('the King of Heroes') emerged victorious against his older brother. Once this man, known to western historians as Xerxes I, had consolidated his grip on power, he turned his attention to conquering those annoying Greeks once and for all.

This time nothing was going to be taken for granted. The Persians would take their time and do it right. The entire power of the empire would be leveraged against Greece, and that unruly land would be subdued less by tactics and generalship than by pure overwhelming force. According to Herodotus over forty nations were commanded to provide men and materiel, and the entire army took four years to muster and prepare.

There was no way that such a slow and massive build-up could go unnoticed by the Greeks. In fact, says Herodotus, the Spartans at least knew exactly what to expect. It will be remembered that the scheming of King Cleomenes had resulted in the Oracle at Delphi being bribed and the legitimacy of King Demaratus thrown into doubt (pp 111-112). Forced into exile from Sparta, Demaratus had eventually been welcomed into the court of King Darius. He was retained by the court of King Xerxes as the expert-in-place of all things Greek and especially of matters Spartan. Since it was in the interest of the Persians that their Spartan advisor be kept up to speed on developments back home, a certain amount of correspondence between Demaratus and friends in Sparta was expected, and even encouraged. Herodotus takes up the tale:

> 'The Spartans were the first to know that Xerxes was preparing to invade Greece. ... They received this information in a strange way. Demaratus the [disputed] son of Ariston was an exile in Persia. I can see no reason why he should feel friendly towards the Lacedaemonians, so the question is whether his actions were inspired by concern for his homeland or a spiteful urge to gloat.
>
> When Xerxes was preparing his invasion Demaratus was at [the Persian capital of] Susa and was aware of what was happening. Fearing detection .... he sent a bearer with a seemingly blank wax tablet which would not arouse the suspicions of inspectors along the way. When the tablet arrived in Sparta, the Spartans were baffled about what

it was for. Finally – so I am told – Gorgo, the daughter of Cleomenes and the wife of Leonidas worked out the trick. She told the Spartans to scrape away the wax and look for writing on the wood backing. When they did so, they found the message [of the Persian invasion plans] and informed the rest of Greece.'

Herodotus *History* 7.239

This anecdote is regarded with some suspicion by historians as it is tacked in a rather ungainly fashion onto the end of Herodotus' Book Seven, and may be a later addendum. In any case, the Greeks needed little warning that a new invasion attempt was on the way. Xerxes had again sent ambassadors demanding earth and water from the Greeks, probably as a way of gauging how much resistance he could expect from the various city-states. He did not even bother asking Athens or Sparta, since there was no point in wasting an ambassador to get the inevitable Spartan reply. Nor was there any point in asking Athens to surrender. From a Persian perspective, that city had gone far beyond forgiveness. One point of the coming invasion was to wipe Athens off the face of the earth.

Given that any opposition to the Persians would therefore form around the Spartan-Athenian alliance, it was, given the fractious nature of the Greek city-states, natural enough that those major cities most opposed to the pair should also be the most sympathetic to Persia. Thus Argos and Thebes were among the 'Persianizers' who indicated that Persia's intention to flatten Athens and Sparta was fine by them. Thessaly later joined this group once the people of that disunited nation saw that they were probably going to fall under Persian rule in any case. Given that Macedonia had already submitted and Thessaly was wavering, the way was clear for a Persian army to advance on the Peloponnese from the north.

Therefore late in 481, the Spartans called a meeting of all states prepared to resist a Persian attack. Diplomatically, they called for the meeting to be held not in Sparta itself but at a place in Laconia later called 'Hellenium' (Paus. 3. 12. 6). Mustering any alliance took some doing. Before the Greeks could agree to stand together against the common enemy there were at least a dozen minor wars going on between the would-be allies that needed to be patched up or at least put temporarily into abeyance. However, Athens and Sparta pulling together made a diplomatic force which was hard to refuse. The Spartan army was renowned for its ferocity, and the Spartans had a deserved reputation for repaying both good deeds and grudges. Athens, meanwhile, had come into a navy.

This stroke of timely good fortune was due to the Athenians unexpectedly striking a vein of rich silver in their mines at Laurium. At first it was proposed that this bounty be divided among the citizens. Then, on more sober reflection it was decided that the money should be used for a state enterprise – namely the building of a large and well-equipped fleet. Originally this was intended to be used to quash that Athenian rival, the island state of Aegina. With the growth of the Persian threat, the Athenian ships were re-purposed to stand off the (reportedly massive) Persian invasion fleet. Meanwhile, the fact that Athens had a large fleet and Sparta had her army made it possible for the two states to lean on waverers and force an end to inter-state feuds. As the only professional soldiers in Greece, the Spartans took the lead in organizing the nation's defence. It was Sparta which chose the leaders of the alliance, and dictated its strategy.

Prelude to the Thermopylae Campaign

By 480 BC, the Persian invasion of Greece was under way. According to Herodotus and his contemporaries, the army of Xerxes was the largest force ever mustered on the planet to date. In fact, the Greeks later claimed in a triumphal inscription that they had stood off an enemy army three million strong. (Herodotus 7.228). Modern historians look with incredulity at the suggestion that the Persians had over a million men on the march, even if that figure includes every warrior, his servants and pack-donkey. According to modern calculations, 200,000, maybe 300,000, would be the best that the Persians could muster, and even 300,000 is a stretch. We can note though, that it is not as if the Greeks were under-informed. The alliance had sent three spies precisely for the purpose of ascertaining the size of the army which was about to descend upon them. When these men were captured by the Persians they were not executed. Instead King Xerxes himself took the time and trouble to show the men around his invasion force and ensured that they took careful notes. He wanted the Greeks to know exactly what they were in for. Therefore any later exaggerations can be blamed on hyperbole, but not on ignorance.

In fact it appears that the Spartan defence strategy was largely based on the very fact that the army of Xerxes was so large, and consequently ungainly and logistically demanding. The Greek commanders noted how long it took for this mass of humanity to roll towards the Hellespont. By the time the Persians could get across and into northern Greece, it would be already late July. Properly speaking, Persians needed to conquer at least a substantial part of Greece by the middle of September, or October at the very latest. Thereafter it would become very difficult for the Persians to keep their massive army in the field, simply because it was a daunting proposition to find food and shelter for that many men over the winter.

Greece was never a particularly fertile land. If the Persian army was even a fraction of the size that the Greeks believed it to be, then the allies needed to ensure that when winter arrived their enemies had not yet conquered anywhere with a decent grain supply. The vicious winter storms of the eastern Mediterranean would then ensure that grain transports would never make it across the Aegean Sea. Lacking supplies, and with extended lines of communication through hostile Thrace, the Persians would be forced to fall back from Greece. Since there was a limited time that even the mighty resources of the Persian Empire could afford to finance so large an army, if the Greeks could keep the Persians off their throats in this campaigning season, it was quite possible that the Persians would not be back for the next.

This seems to have been the thinking behind the original Greek plan which was to hold the Persians at the Vale of Tempe on the mountainous border of Macedonia with Thessaly. As noted earlier, this was extremely rugged and easily defensible terrain. Therefore if the Persians could be stopped here, they could be stopped altogether for it was not likely that the Persians would again opt for the suicidal alternative of taking their fleet around the Athos promontory. However, even as the Greeks were digging in at Tempe, a message came from King Alexander I of Macedon.

Alexander (an ancestor of that Alexander later called 'the Great') was a Persian vassal by necessity rather than choice, and he had no wish to see the rest of Greece share his fate. He advised the Greeks that the position they had chosen was indefensible, for the Persian army could advance through a nearby pass and thus turn their flank. Such were the Persian numbers that it was not possible for the over-stretched Greeks to hold both passes. Once the Spartan commanders had verified this information the defensive project was abandoned. The army returned to its base near Corinth.

According to Herodotus it was at this point that the Thessalians realized that the alliance had now decided to make its stand further south. Therefore they threw in their lot with the Persians who were certain to occupy their land anyway. Though Thessaly had been pro-Persian for some time, this outright defection redoubled diplomatic efforts among the cities further to the south. The Argives came close to being persuaded to join the Pan-Hellenic cause, but the idea that their hoplites would be under Spartan command was too much for them to stomach. After all, the Spartans led by Cleomenes had recently slain the Argives in their thousands, so the Argives baulked at the idea of being under the very commanders who had accomplished this. Eventually a compromise was agreed upon by which Sparta and Argos agreed to cease hostilities for a generation (which in Greek terms was thirty years) and Argos would sit out the Persian Wars on the side-lines.

Thebes also was pressed into the alliance, but joined reluctantly and with very bad grace. So says Herodotus. However, the Boeotian Plutarch, writing many years later, has bitterly criticized the pro-Athenian bias of Herodotus. His treatise *On the Malignity of Herodotus* makes a number of valid points. There is no doubt that Herodotus, writing mainly for an Athenian audience, puts his readers front and centre of the action, and possibly with malice aforethought, makes both the Spartans and Thebans appear dilatory, incompetent and possibly even treacherous. This is also probably why Herodotus does not give us anything resembling a coherent Spartan battle-plan for the defence of Greece, even though the highly competent Spartans undoubtedly had one and Herodotus undoubtedly knew it.

When news arrived in Sparta that King Xerxes and his army had bridged and crossed the Hellespont, it was time to put that plan into operation. There was a complication however, this time introduced by the Oracle at Delphi. As always, the Greeks, and especially the devout Spartans, had diligently sought the guidance of the gods during this dangerous period. For Sparta the Oracle was not particularly encouraging.

'You with homes on the streets of wide Laconia
The children of Perseus shall sack your famous town,
Or failing that, all in the land of Laconia
Must mourn the death of a King,
A descendant of mighty Hercules.
Not the courage of bulls or lions will withstand him [Xerxes]
Try as you might, he has the strength of Zeus
Nothing will stop him from taking as prey
Either your King or your city.'

Herodotus *History* 7.220

Just to complicate things further, the Persians had again arrived just as the Spartans were preparing to celebrate the Karneia. Also this was an Olympic year, and these sacred games caused a further layer of complication. As with Marathon a decade previously, the Spartans were reluctant to commit troops while their religious festivals were under way.

Nevertheless King Leonidas urged the Ephors that it was essential, even should the rest of Sparta do honour to Apollo, that he and a picked force be allowed to head north at once. After all, the last time the Spartans had dallied through the Karneia it had proven to be a public-relations disaster. If they dragged their feet again this time, the disaster would be military, and a lot more substantial. Leonidas urged this, even though he was well aware of the terms of the oracle and that he himself was King and a descendant of Hercules. In other words, Leonidas was aware that he might have to sacrifice himself to save his city.

As a result, and despite the disquiet of the Ephors, Leonidas set out from Sparta during the festival with a picked bodyguard of 300 men. These men were the *hippeis*, but they were not chosen in the usual manner (described on p.128). Instead Leonidas asked for those who had living children, so that when these men fell their family and bloodline would continue.

Battle Plan

If we follow Herodotus' rather cursory account of the Spartan strategy, it would appear that Leonidas and his tiny force threw themselves against the Persian juggernaut rather like a hedgehog under a bus. However modern historians are able to reconstruct what the Greeks actually intended through empirical observation of what actually happened combined with later accounts such as those of Justin and Diodorus (both probably based on the work of a now lost historian called Ephorus). From this it would appear that the Spartan expeditionary force was not originally intended as a suicide mission, though no-one doubted it would be very dangerous. Nor is it now believed that the battle was simply a delaying action to give the Athenians time to evacuate their city before the Persians descended upon it. Rather it appears as though the Greeks were going to attempt to do as they had failed to accomplish at Tempe, and hold the Persians back from the rest of Greece until the winter.

The battle of Thermopylae (the 'hot gates' – a name drawn from the thermal springs nearby) was in fact two battles, and it was not Leonidas in overall command but a Spartan commoner chosen by the Hellenic allies. This man was called Eurybiadas, and he was with the fleet. That the overall commander of this combined operation had chosen to locate himself aboard ship rather than with the land force is a significant indicator of how the Greeks saw the situation unfolding. If the Spartan command had believed that the land battle would be the more significant militarily, Eurybiadas would have positioned himself there – especially as the fleet had a very able second-in-command in the Athenian Themistocles.

We now turn to Herodotus' excellent description of the battleground – a description almost certainly based upon personal observation. This description is all the more vital as time has considerably changed and widened the coastline, so the modern site very little resembles the ancient battlefield.

'The pass at Trachis to [the rest of] Greece is fifty feet wide.

However, this is not where it is narrowest, but further along, before the Hot Gates. Behind that at Alpeni, the route is only as wide as an ox-cart ... To the west there is a high ridge, an outcrop of Mount Oeta, which is so steep as to be inaccessible. To the east, there are bogs and the sea.

Across the route a wall has been raised, which once had a gate in it. ... The Phoceans built this, and because they were trying by every means possible to keep the Thessalians from invading their country, they diverted the hot springs to make a watercourse across the pass. ... The village of Alpeni is right next to the road, and the Greeks intended to get their supplies from there.'

Herodotus *History* 7.176ff

This passage tells us a lot. For a start it tells us why Leonidas did not want a large army with him. Several hundred could hold a path that narrow as well as could 30,000, with the difference that with 30,000 it would be impossible to manoeuvre or bring troops expeditiously up and down the narrow pathways. Secondly, the fact that the Spartans intended to use the village of Alpeni for supplies tells us that they imagined their force would be there for a while.

The Greek fleet consisted of 271 ships, mostly Athenian, and they were situated at nearby Artemesium. (The name comes from a small temple to Artemis which was on the beach.) Artemesium was the aquatic counterpart of Thermopylae, 'where the wide Thracian sea narrows into a strait between the island of Sciathus and the mainland of Magnesia. Down this strait is Artemesium, which is a beach on the coast of Euboea', says Herodotus (ibid).

From these facts historians such as Hammond ('Sparta at Thermopylae' Hammond, N. *Historia*: Bd. 45, H. 1 (1st Qtr., 1996), pp. 1-20) and Evans ('Notes on Thermopylae and Artemesium' Evans, J. *Historia*, Bd. 18, H. 4 (Aug., 1969), pp. 389-406) have been able to reconstruct the Hellenic strategy at which Herodotus only hints. Basically, Thermopylae was intended to be a sea battle.

When the Persian army descended on Thermopylae, it would find a very narrow pass blocked by a wall, and that wall manned by highly motivated, well-armoured and superbly trained hoplites. At this point the numbers of the Persian army would simply not matter, because however many thousands, or hundreds of thousands of men might be in their army, only a few dozen at a time could advance to the battlefront. The Spartans could defend the wall in shifts, and their tiny number would be an actual advantage. Even when the Persian army was not moving it was eating, and supplies last a lot longer for the side that has much fewer men eating them. In fact Herodotus, who had by now inflated the Persian army to some five million strong, remarks that this massive force drank whole rivers dry. In a brief nod to the issue of logistics, he adds, 'I am surprised that the food did not run out.' Indeed. However, if the Persians remained in one place for more than a few days, run out the food certainly would.

Therefore, baffled by the defenders at Thermopylae, Xerxes would have only one option. If he could not get through the pass, he would have to get around it. That meant putting his army on transports and ferrying them past the obstructive Spartans to a point further south where the beach was wider. It was to prevent this that the Hellenic force had drawn up their fleet.

The beauty of Artemesium was that like Thermopylae on land, the strait was too narrow for the Persian fleet to dominate the battle by numbers alone. Without having to worry about their flanks, the Greeks could concentrate on the Persian ships right in front of them, and given the larger triremes of the Athenians and the superior armour and weapons of their marines, the Greeks were hopeful that they could carry the day. Only hopeful, because the Athenian fleet was at this time still new and untried rather than the deadly maritime force it became in later years. Nevertheless, the odds were better at sea; especially as the Persians were of a somewhat landlubberly disposition – as their previous failure to round Athos had demonstrated. Much of the fighting in a sea battle would have to be done by Persia's more nautically-capable subjects, including conscript Greeks from Ionia, and these subjects would probably fight less ferociously than the Persians themselves.

In this context it is significant that the Oracle at Delphi – always well-informed – told the anxious Greeks that they 'should pray to the winds'. The wind would have little effect on a land battle in a narrow pass, but the right winds could be decisive in a battle at sea. In short, it would seem that the Greeks were reasonably confident that Leonidas and his elite team could hold the pass at Thermopylae while the real issue was decided at sea. It can therefore be assumed that it was uncertainty of the outcome of the sea battle which caused the Athenians to issue the well-known 'Trozen decree' which prepared the citizens for the evacuation of their city should the attempt to hold back the Persians fail.

Battle

Hostilities started at sea, with an engagement between the Persian fleet and Boreas, the north wind. The Athenians had chosen a location sheltered from the wind by the landmass on either side of their strait, and being weather-wise, they recognised the signs of a type of storm so common that it had a name – the 'Hellespontium'. In this storm the seas were raised in a confused mass as though the water was boiling in a massive cauldron. There was no chance of riding it out, and any Persian ships unable to run ashore and secure themselves were lost.

The battle with the storm was costly to the Persian fleet, with victory going to Boreas who sank 400 warships and 'uncountable' minor vessels and transport. At a very rough estimate this meant that the Persians still outnumbered the Greeks around 3-1 at sea. Nevertheless, the odds had shortened considerably, and Greek morale soared at this proof of the protection of the gods. It also made Xerxes all the more determined to keep his army on land and to force his way through Thermopylae if this was at all possible.

Back to Herodotus –

'While still in Thessaly Xerxes had heard that Thermopylae was occupied by a small force led by the Spartans and Leonidas, the descendant of Hercules. Accordingly he sent a mounted scout to see how many there were in this force and what they were doing. So the horseman rode up to the Spartan encampment to see what he could of the place. He could not see over the wall, which the Spartans had rebuilt and guarded. He did however note that there were Spartans outside who had stacked their kit against the wall. Some of these were exercising naked, and others were combing out their hair. Since no-one attempted to chase him away, or paid him any attention at all, the amazed scout was able to take careful note of the men and their numbers and ride back at his leisure to report to Xerxes.

When Xerxes heard this … he sent for Demaratus the son of Ariston, who was in his camp, because he was unable to understand what the Spartans thought they were doing.

Demaratus said, "I make it my highest intention, Sir, to always tell you the truth. When we set out on this expedition I told you about the Spartans and of how this might go. When you heard you mocked me, so I will tell you again. The Spartans have come to fight and hold the pass, and that is what they are preparing to do. It is their custom to groom their hair before battle. You are now attacking the best men of the toughest state in Greece. Be certain that if you can overwhelm these men and their countrymen, no-one else will dare to raise a hand against you."

Xerxes was incredulous, and asked how such a tiny force could dare to take on his entire army. Demaratus replied, 'My King, if I am wrong you can punish me as a liar, but things will turn out as I have said.'

Herodotus History 7.207ff.

With the massive Persian army now gearing up for the assault, Leonidas actually sent away most of the troops with him.

How many these troops actually were is a much-disputed issue. When he started from Sparta, Leonidas had with him his 300 *hippei*, and as well as this bodyguard, (probably) 1,000 Lacedaemonian *perioiki* and around 900 helot auxiliaries. As he had gone northward, Leonidas had picked up a motley array of reinforcements. These included 400 Thebans, and another 400 from the small city of Thespis. Local Phoceans and Locrians had contributed to the force, though how many men is uncertain (for the Locrians, Herodotus says merely that they sent 'everyone they had').

Overall, we might assume that Leonidas had around 7,000 men. Of these, the Spartan king decided to dispense with over half. The Phoceans remained as light troops holding the hills west and above the pass. The helots stayed to act as support troops for the Spartans and the Thebans were kept well back as a reserve. Smaller contingents from the other cities also remained.

By now the king must have studied the ground and decided that the pass could either be held by 300, or it could not be held at all. If it could not be held, then there was no point in wasting troops who would later be needed elsewhere. If Thermopylae could be held, then the best available people to do it were already on the job. Not that the Spartans were alone at this point – Leonidas intended his Spartiates to take the brunt of the attacks and then to rotate other Greek contingents in and out of the pass depending on the pressure upon them.

On the Persian side, Xerxes was still uncertain that this tiny force was serious about standing off his massive army. Accordingly he sent ambassadors to persuade the Greeks to surrender and hand over their weapons and armour. To this Leonidas replied in true laconic style, '*molon labe*' - 'come and take them'. (Plutarch, *Sayings of the Spartans* 51.11)

After five days, it became clear that the Spartan morale was going to outlast declining Persian food-stocks, and a frustrated and infuriated Xerxes had no choice but to attempt to move the Spartans by force. His opening salvo was just that – volley after volley of arrows fired in the knowledge that the Spartans had no missile troops with which to retaliate, so they could only hunker down and take it.

The Spartans were expecting this. Before the battle veterans from the city of Trachis had warned one of the Spartans – an officer called Dienekes - that 'the arrows from the king's army fly so thickly that they darken the sun'. Cheerfully, Dienekes had reported back to his comrades the good news that 'it appears we shall be fighting in the shade.' Such insouciance proved justified. Sheltered by their wall and heavy armour, the warrior hoplites simply hefted their large shields over their heads and sat out the storm of arrows as though it were a simple rainstorm. Compared to the effort and arrows expended, casualties were light.

Observing that his bowmen were gaining little apart from healthy exercise, Xerxes sent his infantry into the fray. The first wave was basically to see what the Spartans could do and the Spartans obligingly demonstrated their capability by chopping the attackers to pieces. Xerxes increased the stakes by sending in his top-quality Medean infantry. The Spartans appeared to turn tail before this more formidable attack, causing Xerxes to leap to his feet. He sat down again when the Spartans revealed that this manoeuvre was intended to cause the Medes to break formation. Once the ploy succeeded, the Spartans turned on the disorganized enemy and chopped them to bits as well. Finally, Xerxes sent forward the elite troops of his army, the 10,000 'Immortals'. These too achieved little other than to prove that their name was technically incorrect.

Rebuffed on land, Xerxes sent his fleet forward to see if the maritime option looked any more promising. While he was at it, he sent a large contingent of ships around the entire island of Euboea (which made up the eastern part of the strait the Athenians were defending). The idea was that these ships would finally turn up behind the Athenian fleet and bottle it into the strait. It was a cunning plan, but one which failed to take into account late summer storms and the lamentable Persian inability to deal with them. The inevitable storm was followed by another collection of shipwrecks on the exposed lee shore of Euboea, and the Athenian rear remained secure.

With the Athenian fleet as obdurate as the Spartan hoplites, Xerxes had little choice but to keep hammering away at both throughout the next day, in the hope that sheer weariness and wounds would finally cause his enemy to collapse. Some progress was made at sea – the Athenians were battering the lighter Persian ships and had captured some thirty of these, but they too were being worn down. However, by way of compensation a further fifty-three ships arrived from Athens that day which more than compensated for their losses.

Xerxes might have contemplated a third day of battle with considerable gloom. So far the irresistible Persian force had achieved very little against the Greek immovable object, and it looked as though little was going to change. Perhaps his army would be stymied at Thermopylae after all. At this point, a local called Ephialtes decided to change history. He approached Xerxes and informed him that, for a very large sum of money, he would show the Persians a little-known path that would take the Persians around the Spartans at Thermopylae. Predictably, Xerxes leapt at the chance, and Ephialtes was dispatched to guide a large force of picked men that very night.

The third day of the Persian attack began ominously for Greece.

Alerted by the sound of the Persians moving through an oak grove, the Phoceans came to arms. Seeing a large Persian force heading for them, the Phoceans hurried to make a stand on a nearby hill – not an unreasonable move if the Phoceans assumed that the Persians intended to attack them and the defenders were outnumbered twenty-to-one. The Persians, though, had bigger fish to fry, so they simply treated the Phoceans to a brisk volley of arrows and moved on. The dismayed Phoceans sent an urgent message to Leonidas informing him that the flank of his defensive position had been turned, and with a large Persian force in behind it, Thermopylae was now indefensible.

In short, thanks to the traitor Ephialtes, Xerxes had done by land what he had failed to achieve by sea. He had got a large part of his army around the bottleneck at Thermopylae, and was now poised to attack central Greece. This did not stop the Persian King from seeing how a further test of naval strength would go, and his ships advanced on the Athenian triremes even as his army closed in on the Greek hoplites.

With the changed situation in mind, Leonidas made some hasty re-deployments. From the moment he received the news from the Phoceans, he seems to have accepted that Delphi was going to have its due, and a Spartan king would be sacrificed. Perhaps Leonidas drew solace from looking up at Mount Oeta, where his ancestor Hercules had died, aware that in a sense, he too would be joining the immortals that day. Grimly he informed his men, 'Eat a good breakfast, lads. Dinner will be served in the afterlife.'

It remains an open question whether some of the other Greek contingents simply fled (as Herodotus alleges) or whether they were ordered to withdraw to be useful later. The Spartans remained, as did the contingent from Thespis, and surprisingly, the Thebans. Leonidas ordered one of his men to leave with these departees to tell the Ephors in Sparta what had happened. (Another indication that Thermopylae was never meant to be a suicide mission from the start. If all had been going to plan there would have been no need to inform the folks back home of the fact.) In a rare act of insubordination to a superior, the designated Spartan refused to go. He growled that he was a warrior, not a messenger boy, and returned to the ranks of the doomed hoplites.

It remained true that though Thermopylae was certain to be lost, the pass still had to be held for as long as possible. Now Athens did need to be evacuated, and nearby Thespis too – which explains why the Thespian contingent chose to sacrifice themselves and remain. Every hour gained would help the evacuation to succeed. It would also help those Greek soldiers hastily departing the scene, since Persian cavalry could otherwise catch up with them, ride the smaller contingents down, or force the larger ones into defensive formations until the Persian army caught up.

Xerxes realized that even now, Leonidas intended to hold the pass, and so he ordered his army forward. With the enemy also at their backs, there was no reason for the Greeks to stay at the wall. They advanced to meet the enemy head-on in a ferocious last stand. The pass was still narrow, and the Spartans were more than a match for their opponents. This did not really matter, because Xerxes had an almost endless supply of replacements to throw into the fight. Eventually the Spartan spears were shattered, so they switched to their swords. The men who lost these fought on 'with their fingers and teeth', or so Herodotus tells us.

In this last bloody melee, Leonidas was killed and a still more intense and bloody fight developed for possession of his body. The Spartans won, but by now they were too few to hold the line. The overall Greek army was even fewer also, because in a lull in the fighting the entire Theban contingent abruptly surrendered to the Persians *en masse*. A few were killed before the Persians were convinced that this capitulation was genuine, and a contemptuous Xerxes later ordered that the remaining Theban prisoners be branded with the Persian royal seal.

The rest of the Greeks withdrew to a small hill near the beach and prepared to fight to the death. Xerxes was well aware that there would be a substantial number of Persian deaths if he obliged the Greek desire for a final round of hand-to-hand combat. Instead he ordered his archers forward, and again thousands of Persian arrows darkened the sun. This time there was no wall to shelter the Spartans, and many had lost their shields. Modern archaeology has identified the hill on which the Greeks made their last stand, because even today the site is saturated with Persian arrowheads. No bodies were found, because once they had regained possession of the site the people of Greece gave the corpses a heroes' funeral.

It says something of the scare that the usually chivalrous Xerxes had been given by the stubborn defence that the King took out his rage and relief on the slain body of Leonidas. He had the corpse beheaded, and the leftovers crucified. Then tearing down the wall, his army advanced on central Greece.

Meanwhile, the navy at Artemesium had fought the Persians to a standstill. It was a bruising day for both sides, and casualties were about equal. However, given the numerical superiority of the Persian fleet, this meant that the odds had lengthened against the Athenians. The commanders were debating whether to attempt to hold for another day or retreat when news arrived of the disaster at Thermopylae. Realizing that the attempt to hold the Persians back had failed, the fleet withdrew to help with the evacuation of Athens. Once Thermopylae had fallen, it was certain that Athens would also be taken by the Persians.

Given that the Greeks had failed to hold Thermopylae, the battle was a defeat. Had Xerxes been held for a few days longer, it might have been a stunning victory that kept Greece safe for another decade. The wretched Ephialtes received most of the blame. His name later became a byword for treachery, but the truth was that the Athenian fleet was so dilapidated from hard fighting that it would barely have lasted another day anyway. The Persian fleet was simply too large and powerful, and once it had forced the Athenians aside, Thermopylae was doomed in any case.

In another sense, Thermopylae was a glorious victory. History has edited out the equally heroic contribution of the Thespians, and made the Spartans the heroes of the day. Today the battle is seen as the triumph of the spirit of free men against slavery – though one wonders what the Messenian helots who also died on the battlefield might have thought of that. Thermopylae and the self-sacrifice of Leonidas also came to epitomize what it was to be Spartans – heroic, unflinching and even cheerful in the face of certain death, willing to give up their lives for the greater good.

Today a statue of Leonidas stands at the pass he guarded so

faithfully, where in antiquity the Greeks had placed a stone lion.
Yet the more durable memorial has been the simple epitaph later
written by Simonides of Kos.

Go tell the Spartans, passer-by
We obeyed our orders - and here we lie.

Chapter Twelve

Apogee

With defeat at Thermopylae, Sparta faced a choice – should the Spartans fall back on their heartland of Lacedaemon, defend that, and leave the rest of Greece to come to what terms it could with the Persians? Or should the Spartans continue to take the lead in the pan-Greek alliance and concentrate on driving the Persians out of Hellas altogether?

Certainly Sparta was hedging its bets. At its narrowest, the Isthmus of Corinth is 6.3km (4 miles) across, and here the Spartans were hastily building a defensive wall, enthusiastically assisted by the other peoples of the Peloponnese. With progress on the wall, falling back on the Peloponnese was rapidly becoming a viable option. Thereafter, if the Persians wanted to take the Peloponnese in a land assault, the ensuing battle would be a repeat of Thermopylae on a grand scale.

King Xerxes had little taste for such an encounter. Leonidas had taught him a healthy respect for what a Spartan hoplite could do when entrenched in a secure position. Fortunately, on the Peloponnese, as with Thermopylae, there was no need to go through the Spartans when one could go around them. Indeed ex-king Demaratus was hoping to make a Spartan nightmare come true by urging the Persians to occupy the island of Kythera just off Cape Malea. With Laconia thus under threat, the Spartans would be forced to abandon the rest of Greece. In fact, the occupation of Kythera might even force the Spartans to terms, whereafter the rest of Greece would collapse like a cheap tent in a wind-storm.

Even without Kythera, the Peloponnese was a peninsula with numerous locations where a sizeable army could be landed, provided that Persian transports were free to do so. And that was the problem. Despite the bruising encounter at Artemesium, the allied Greek fleet remained largely intact. If the Persian army had learned to respect Spartan hoplites, the Athenian triremes now evoked a matching degree of caution in the Persian navy.

Therefore until the Athenian navy was taken out of the picture, Persia's transports could not take the army anywhere, let alone on the dangerous voyage to the Peloponnese.

There was another complication. The campaigning season was fast coming to an end, and Xerxes was a king in a hurry. For a start, he still had to find provisions with which to feed his massive army through the winter, and the Athenian fleet was also a risk to grain shipments from Asia. Secondly, the ruler of a kingdom that stretched to the banks of the River Indus in the east simply could not spend too much time beyond the bounds of the western frontier of his empire. At least not if he wanted to keep ruling the rest of it. Xerxes needed to get back to his capital and pick up the reigns of governance soon, before someone else decided to do it for him.

As a result of these considerations, after Thermopylae the Persians moved south as hastily as possible. The little city of Thespis was devastated for its defiance of Persia, and Plataea followed (the Persians at least, remembered the Plataean contribution to Marathon). Athens was the next horrible example. The Oracle at Delphi had warned the Athenians to trust in their 'wooden walls'. While most Athenians decided correctly that this meant the wooden hulls of their triremes, some diehards decided to shelter behind wooden walls on the Athenian Acropolis – and die hard they did. Athens came under Persian control, though the Persians had little interest in occupying the city. As the Athenians had done to the Persian provincial capital of Sardis, Athens was burned to the ground. As a further punishment, the city walls were thrown down. However, this did not destroy Athens. The physical location had been flattened, but the Athenian people had already been safely evacuated to the island of Salamis, and the Athenian fleet was still very much alive.

Thebes, never an enthusiastic member of the anti-Persian alliance, saw the writing on the now-destroyed walls of Athens, and offered Persia the surrender of Boeotia. This surrender gave Xerxes a winter base, although he had to keep his army on the move to avoid stripping local areas of their food supply. His army was still unsustainably large, the campaigning season was running out, and Sparta remained as undefeated as ever.

Fortunately for Xerxes, it appeared that there was disunity amongst his enemies.

The base of the Greek alliance was now the island of Salamis, and opinions there were divided. It appeared that the Peloponnesians, led by Sparta, wanted to go home. The Athenians were naturally keen on keeping the fleet together and taking on the Persians as soon as possible. Both positions were understandable. The Spartans were justifiably worried that the Persian proximity to Messenia might provoke a rebellion, and they wanted their army to be on hand to nip trouble in the bud before they had to take on the Persians and Messenians together. There was also Argos to consider. If Sparta got into serious trouble while fighting on two fronts, then Argive honour would be severely tested by the temptation to abandon the truce with Sparta and join in the fray to finish off the city's hated enemy. Finally, there was the succession issue to handle, for Sparta had lost a king and with him 300 Spartans from leading families.

The Athenians on the other hand had a city and homeland under Persian occupation, and they felt that getting the enemy off their territory should be everyone's first concern. As the Athenians never stopped reminding the Spartans it was Athenian triremes that were keeping the Peloponnese safe from invasion.

The Battle of Salamis – and the Aftermath

Xerxes had a front-row seat in the debate, as the wily Themistocles made sure that the King was kept well-informed. Themistocles had correctly deduced that Xerxes wanted the chance to smash the allied fleet with one blow. The Persian simply did not have the time to go chasing after the Athenian and Peloponnesian contingents separately. Therefore when Xerxes received advance notification that the fleet was going to split up into its separate factions, the King reacted immediately by ordering his fleet into the strait of Salamis to defeat the enemy ships while they were in a single fleet.

Afterwards, naturally enough, everyone insisted that the alleged disunity among the allies was simply a cunning pretence designed to force Xerxes to fight under conditions which favoured the Greeks. How real the disagreement truly was is something which no-one would talk about at the time, and something which certainly cannot be discovered over 2,000 years later. Certainly, when they realized that battle was inevitable, the Peloponnesians accepted the fact without hesitation and fought whole-heartedly.

The result was a stunning Greek victory. The lighter Persian fleet was channelled into the narrow Salamis strait where the heavy Athenian ships had the advantage. In open water the more agile Persian ships would have outmanoeuvred the Greeks and swarmed them with sheer numbers. This was not possible in the confined waters off Salamis, which is precisely why the Greeks had wanted to fight there. For a long time the battle was close, with Queen Artemesia of Halicarnassus and her ships performing heroics for the Persian cause. Nevertheless, in a head-to-head fight the better armed and armoured Greek marines were able to defeat an enemy who, just as at Thermopylae, were unable to bring their superior numbers to bear. Eventually the Persians were forced to pull back, and as they did so, they ran into an ambush of Aegientan ships, as the people of Aegina had concluded that they were better off outside the Persian Empire.

Overall, the Persians lost somewhere between a third to a half of their fleet (since the numbers of the Persian fleet have never been satisfactorily established, the proportion must remain also inexact). The Greeks lost forty ships, a figure also open to question, as the Athenians appear to have been in the habit of underestimating their casualties. What is undisputed is that Salamis completely changed the complexion of the war, and quite possibly the course of history.

For a start, with the Persian fleet mauled and the Athenian triremes now masters of the sea, there was no question of Xerxes invading the Peloponnese. Instead, much of the Persian army would have to pull out of Greece altogether. The land could not support both the massive Persian army and the local people, and grain convoys could not supply the army by sea due to the threat of winter weather and the marauding Athenian navy. Accordingly Xerxes and a large part of his army withdrew to Asia Minor. The remainder of the army in Greece was left under the command of Mardonius, that same commander who had overseen the Persian defeat at Marathon. Having seen the Greeks fighting at first-hand, Xerxes was now more sympathetic to what Mardonius had faced. He probably decided it was better to leave his army with someone who had already learned the hard lessons about hoplite warfare than with an inexperienced and consequently over-confident general.

For the Spartans, victory at Salamis was cause for rejoicing, but also for disquiet. For a start it was yet another famous victory over the Persians which had been won by people who were not Spartans. Thermopylae, when one came right down to it, was a defeat. Marathon and Salamis were mainly Athenian victories. Of these, Salamis was particularly concerning. True, the Spartan Eurybiadas had been nominally in command of the fleet, but the victory had been engineered by the Athenian Themistocles and won by Athenian ships. Consequently the Athenians could claim that their efforts had prevented the invasion of the Peloponnese, and that they had thus saved the Spartans. This was not something that a nation based upon military prowess liked to think about.

It may well be that it was after Salamis that the Spartans began to think that eventually something was going to have to be done about Athens. The Athenians were developing a competence in matters military which was disturbing in a culture so different to the Spartan. The Spartans were conservative – in fact rigidly so. The Athenians were not only open-minded and receptive to new ideas, but if enough new ideas were not forthcoming they had plenty of their own to fill the gap. The Athenians were experimenters and innovators, while the Spartans liked things just as they were. The latest Athenian experiment was with radical democracy, and this the Spartans heartily disliked.

While Sparta was technically a democracy, or at least a government of 'equals', it was accepted that some Spartan families were more equal than others. Spartans understood that for a person to rule he should first accept being ruled by others. This was acceptable. In Athens though, that ruler might be a shoemaker, a merchant or anyone else selected by – of all things – a lottery, rather than by measured deliberation among the great and good. This was not acceptable.

While Athens was a lesser state, this eccentricity was perhaps tolerable. But Salamis and Marathon had raised Athens to the first rank of Greek military powers, almost on a par with Sparta itself. The Spartans might have had major reservations about this fact, but frustratingly, they could not do anything about it right now. If the Persian threat was to be contained, Athens and Sparta needed each other.

Sparta after Thermopylae

Sparta's conservative, defensive approach to the Persian wars was partly due to the fact that Persian invaders were not the only major threat facing the city. Unlike the Athenians who could throw themselves whole-heartedly into the campaign, the Spartans had constantly to remain also prepared for a helot revolt or an opportunistic Argive assault. To compound the issue, the successor to the heroically slain King Leonidas was his son Pleistarchus, who was too young to rule in his own right. Over the next few months this led to jockeying among various factions among the Spartan elite as to who should exercise power in the young king's name.

That debate was won by Pausanias, a cousin just outside the line of succession, and as later events were to prove, rather bitter about this fact. Nevertheless, for the moment at least, Pausanias had the powers, if not the name of king and he intended to make the most of it.

The Spartan people as a whole reacted to the defeat at Thermopylae with immense pride at the defiance which the 300 had shown. But if Leonidas had shown the best of what it meant to be Spartan, the treatment of the survivors of that battle showed the worst.

Two men, Eurytus and Aristodemus, had been stricken with illness before the battle. Eurytus, though almost blinded by ophthalmia, demanded his armour and was led to the battle by a helot. Being unable to see what he was doing, he was cut down rather swiftly. Meanwhile Aristodemus had 'lost his strength' (says Herodotus, who does not say whether this loss was physical or moral), and remained on his sickbed and so missed the fight.

'When Aristodemus came back to Sparta, he was disgraced and dishonoured. Everyone considered him as having no self-respect, and so no Spartan would give him fire, or speak to him except to insult him with the name of Aristodemus the Trembler.'

Herodotus *History* 7.231

Then there was Pantites, a Spartan who obeyed his orders and took a message to Thessaly. The battle took place while he was gone, but this was considered an insufficient excuse. When he returned to Sparta, Pantites was hounded and bullied for not being among the noble dead. Finally he hanged himself.

This attitude, deplorable as it might be, at least showed that the Spartan public were now fully committed to the war. The worry for Sparta's leaders was that the Athenians might not be. Mardonius was well aware of the importance of Athens and its fleet in the war as a whole, and he did his best to split Athens away from the anti-Persian alliance. While his army was away, some Athenians came over the winter to re-settle amid the rubble of their former homes. To these men Mardonius sent Alexander of Macedon, whom he reckoned the most sympathetic emissary he could find.

Alexander's message was two-fold. Firstly, he argued that the power of Persia was massive and irresistible. Secondly he pointed to himself as an example of the fact that assimilation into the Persian Empire was no terrible fate. The Persians were tolerant and easy-going rulers. Simply submit on the very reasonable terms offered, argued Alexander, and life could go on very much as it had before, except that the Athenians would no longer be able to go on freebooting raids to Asia Minor and generally disrupt life for people elsewhere around the Aegean Sea.

The Spartans hastily sent their own emissaries. They pointed out that it was exactly the Athenian freebooting spirit which had got Greece into the current mess, and this mess now involved Sparta through no fault of that city's own. If the Spartans, who had not precipitated the war, were now fully committed to see it through to the end, then the Athenians too should be prepared to finish what they had started. As an incentive, the Spartans added that they were prepared to house and support the Athenian women and non-combatants for as long as the war lasted.

Alexander was rebuffed, but the threat of defection meant that Athens was in a position to dictate Greek strategy. There was a strong sentiment in Sparta that the Greeks should dig into the Peloponnese and let the Persians come to them. This Athens refused to allow. The result was deadlock for several months, with Sparta giving lip service to liberating Athens, but actually keeping to a policy of masterful inactivity. Eventually, angered by the fact that the Spartan army continued to do nothing but fortify the Isthmus, a reproachful embassy came from the Athenians. This embassy pointed out that the campaigning season was nearing its end. It was now August and the Spartans had made no move against the Persians.

> 'The Persian king has offered to return our country to us. He now wants nothing more than an open and equal alliance on fair and honest terms.' (Mardonius had improved his offer after the Athenians rejected those presented by Alexander.)
>
> It is now vastly more advantageous for us to make peace with the Persians than to keep fighting. Despite this, we are not going to make peace if we can help it. That would be a betrayal, and we are keeping fairly to the terms of our alliance. You on the other hand, having found us steadfast to our alliance, are no longer afraid that we will come to terms with the enemy.
>
> Furthermore, now that your wall across the Isthmus is almost complete, you have ceased to care what happens to us. It was agreed that we would advance and meet the Persians in Boeotia – you betrayed your word. … Now send out your army, and let us confront Mardonius.
>
> Herodotus *History* 9.8

Even in the face of an Athenian ultimatum, the Ephors dithered. They promised to give the Athenians an answer the next day, then put it off to the next, and then the next. So it went on for a fortnight until the frustrated Athenians announced their intention to abandon their embassy.

At this point a Tegean named Chileus pointed out to the Ephors the unpalatable fact that they had been refusing to face. If the Athenians followed through with their threat to ally with Persia, then not only would the Athenian fleet not defend the Peloponnese against Persian invaders, but those same triremes that now kept the Spartans safe would be spearheading the attack against them. The wall across the Isthmus would be irrelevant if the Persians could land on any beach they pleased. It was a persuasive argument – so persuasive that when the Athenians came to bid their farewells the next day, they were informed that a Spartan army of 5,000 men had left the city overnight. The ultimatum had called the Spartan bluff, and the decisive battle of the war would be fought in the north.

The Battle of Plataea

In the absence of any other source, the account of events above is derived from Herodotus, and Herodotus was writing for an Athenian audience that was not very fond of Sparta. A more sympathetic writer might have argued that it was always the Spartan intention to fight for Attica as promised. The Spartans, after all, placed a lot of value on their promises.

Seen in this light, the frantic work on the wall across the Isthmus makes more sense. It assumes that the cautious Spartans envisaged a scenario where they went north, were defeated and had to fall back on the Peloponnese once more. Since a land battle would not damage the navy, the wall ensured that Greek bolt-hole would remain secure while the allies regrouped for their next attempt. If the wall was not ready before the Spartans went north this could lead to disaster. Then, if the Spartan force was defeated, the pursuing Persians would flood through the Isthmus, past Corinth into the Argolid. Argos would promptly, even enthusiastically, surrender and it would be game over for Greece. Therefore another view of the situation sees the Ephors diplomatically reining in the childishly impatient Athenians until all the strategic blocks were in place for a safe advance northward. With the wall complete, the army would have advanced with or without the Athenian ultimatum.

We will never know the true story here, but the incontestable fact is that the Spartans did – eventually – do as promised and march northward to fight Mardonius for the freedom of Greece.

Sparta was certainly not going to fight alone. The 5,000 Spartiates were joined by 5,000 *perioiki* and (says Herodotus) around 35,000 helots, making the Lacedaemonian army 45,000 strong. (Whether the helots were to be used as auxiliary troops, reserves or were simply a way of getting the most dangerous potential rebels out of Messenia to somewhere the army could keep an eye on them is unknown. It is significant though, that the Spartans reckoned as a rule of thumb that each Spartan hoplite should be prepared to beat eight Messenian helots – and that was pretty much the proportion of helots to hoplites that the Spartans took to war with them.)

To this the Athenians added 8,000 hoplites of their own, as well as a small contingent of archers. With the Athenians came the Plataeans, few in number but grimly determined to continue their feud with the mighty Persian Empire. Corinth added another 5,000 hoplites and many smaller states sent contingents of under a 1,000 men. As with the Lacedaemonians, we can assume that these hoplite armies from other city-states were accompanied by a swarm of light infantry irregulars. However, to the snobbish Greek historians it was only hoplites that really counted.

Consequently, because the Greeks ignored their own light troops but certainly counted every Persian warrior (and may well have counted several twice over), the numerical superiority of the Persian army remaining in Greece was probably an illusion. The Greeks had, by modern estimates, around 80-100,000 men; about a third of whom were hoplites. This was by far the largest Greek army ever assembled, and probably equalled the size of the Persian force, which Herodotus (over)estimates at 300,000, and the later historian Diodorus Siculus bumps up to 500,000 by adding pretty much the entire male citizenry of subject Greek states such as the Thebans and Thessalians.

All the estimates of troop numbers agree on one thing. The Persians had lots of cavalry – good cavalry too – while the Greek numbers in this arm of warfare were negligible to none. Therefore any confrontation would be based on Mardonius trying to make maximum use of his cavalry and on the Greeks trying to negate this.

The Spartans had naturally put one of their own in charge of the Greek force, and so accustomed by now were the Greeks to Spartan leadership that no-one argued. Thus the overall Greek commander was Pausanias – that cousin who was acting as regent to the young son of the dead Leonidas.

The initial clash was a battle of strategy between Pausanias and Mardonius. As the Greek force advanced, Mardonius gave ground. This was not because he feared a confrontation, but he wanted it to happen on the plains of Boeotia where he could use his cavalry. With the same consideration in mind, as Pausanias advanced he kept his army to the hills. In this manner the Greek and Persian armies kept up a complicated dance that finished sometime in late August, 479 BC in the foothills of the Cithaeron Range, not far from the site of now-destroyed Plataea.

Mardonius was very familiar with the problems of keeping a large army in the field, and he suspected that the Greeks, who had never before mustered an army so large, were going to grapple with their logistics. The Greeks on the hills were unassailable, for Mardonius knew well the suicidal folly of leading his men to attack hoplites in entrenched positions. However, hills are not particularly good sources of food or water, and anyone bringing these supplies to the Greek army had to cross open ground to get there. This is where the Persian cavalry came in. The Persian intention was to cut the Greek supply lines and let hunger and thirst do their fighting for them.

The next few days saw the Greeks holding their position and waiting hopefully for the Persians to attack them. Instead the Persian cavalry scoured the approach lines to the Greek positions and intercepted at least two Greek resupply convoys. From their position, the Greeks had an excellent view of the River Asopus, but the waters of that river were as unapproachable as those of the River Styx. The Persians were camped right against the river, and their archers and cavalry would make short work of any water-bearers. Instead the Greeks relied on a single mountain spring for their water supplies.

Once Mardonius became aware of this – there were plenty of Persian sympathizers in the Greek ranks – he launched a cavalry raid that blocked the spring. Without food or water, the comprehensively out-generalled Pausanias had no choice but to abandon his position. Here again Pausanias' weakness as a general showed clearly. His intention was to retreat toward the remains of the city of Plataea itself, for that city's founders had evidently possessed an eye for safe lines of communication and a good water supply. However, any general knows that a phased withdrawal in the face of the enemy is one of the hardest manoeuvres to successfully accomplish. Pausanias decided to make the attempt more challenging by doing it by night, with a multi-national force that had never worked together before, in an army of a size that no Greek had previously commanded. The result, to use a modern military expression, was organized chaos. (Which differs from normal chaos by being more chaotic.)

Come dawn, the bemused Persians awoke to find the Greek army scattered in untidy blocks between the hills, the plain, and Plataea. Some Greek units had successfully formed up in front of the city, others were *en route* and the Spartan rear-guard had not yet even moved from the hills. To Mardonius it looked as though he had got his enemy exactly where he wanted them – scattered, disorganized and vulnerable. Hastily he ordered his army to move in for the kill.

First to be caught were the Athenians. They were one of the units 'twixt and between city and hills, so Pausanias ordered them back to join the Spartans who were standing their ground near a hilltop temple to the corn-goddess Demeter. The Spartans (and the Tegeans who were with them) were about to be in trouble, for Mardonius had already launched his cavalry against them. The Persian cavalry were not attempting to seriously engage the Spartans, because the Spartans in formation would have massacred them. Their intention was to keep the Spartans pinned until the main body of the Persian army could advance to take them on.

Seeing the Athenians on their way to help the Spartans, Mardonius initiated the first infantry clash of the battle by ordering his Theban allies to intercept the Athenian phalanx. With Athenians and Thebans locked in battle, Mardonius was free to tackle the Spartans and Tegeans without interruption. He started by treating the Spartans to several volleys of bow-fire by way of softening them up, and then sent his elite Persian infantry into the fray. The Spartans had suffered from the volleys of arrows, but could not yet engage the enemy because their commander was sacrificing, and the gods refused to grant their blessing on the day.

A good number of goats and Spartans died before the pious Pausanias found a deity – Hera, as it happened – who was prepared to give favourable omens. In the nick of time the

Spartans could now advance to meet the approaching Persian infantry.

> 'The Persians discarded their bows and met the Spartan counter-charge. The melee started at the Persian shield-fence [the Persian archers had large wicker shields which they inserted into the ground as a barrier against return missile fire.] Once the shields were down, the battle moved to around the temple of Demeter, where it raged for a considerable time. The fighting was at close quarters, for the Persians seized on the spears of the phalanx and broke them off.
>
> Certainly the Persians were as brave as the Greeks, and just as strong. But they were unarmoured and had no training at this type of combat. They rushed at the Spartan lines singly, in handfuls or groups of various sizes, and were cut down … what harmed them most was the lack of armour. They had only their clothes, which was the same as if they were fighting naked against men in full armour.'
>
> Herodotus *History* 9.60-63

Mardonius, riding a distinctive white horse, was close to the forefront of the action, surrounded by his elite troops. The Persian general was aware that his men were outmatched, but also well aware that the bulk of his army was taking on the Spartan contingent alone. If his army could overwhelm the Spartans by sheer numbers then the rest of the disorganized Greek army could be defeated unit by unit. The question was how long the Spartans could keep going until sheer exhaustion ground them down. Then Mardonius made an error. So intent was he on keeping his men pressing forward that he pressed too far forward himself.

> 'As it turned out, the Lacedaemonians were first to repulse the Persians. This happened because Mardonius was killed by a Spartan called Arimnestus, who hurled a stone which crushed his head.'
>
> Plutarch *Aristides* 19

Mardonius was felled by the blow and toppled from his horse.

His presence had been driving his men onward, and without him the attack wilted. Energized, the Spartans pressed forward, and discovered that one advantage of fighting on a hilltop was once you had the enemy going backward, it was downhill all the way. The Persians did not stop retreating until they were safe within the stockade that they had built around their camp on the River Asopus. The Spartans were not very good at taking fortified structures, so at this point they paused for a well-deserved rest while they worked out what to do next.

Meanwhile the Athenians had seen off the Theban phalanx. Though Herodotus denies it, it is probable that Plutarch is correct that the Thebans, like the other conscript Greek allies of the Persians, were not trying very hard. After they had put in somewhat more than a token effort they pulled back. The Athenians, perhaps out of appreciation of the situation the Thebans found themselves in, declined to follow up and so force the Thebans to fight in earnest. Instead the Athenian phalanx went to join the Spartans and the more interesting situation at the stockade.

Athenian ingenuity combined with Spartan fortitude gave a brief demonstration that, if the two states had ever managed to submerge their differences and work together for the long term, the future of Greece might have been very different. As it was, the collaboration in the very short term brought about the fall of the stockade defences. The Persians fought stubbornly while their walls were intact, but suffered heavy casualties when the Greeks finally got in. The Greek victory was complete.

Aftermath

By nightfall, what had been a Persian army dedicated to the conquest of Greece had become a mass of frightened, disorganized groups of Persians engaged in a long-distance jog back to the Hellespont. Only two factors prevented the Persian defeat from becoming a general massacre. One is that a certain Artabazus and 40,000 of his infantry had not been involved in the battle – either because of this officer's distrust of Mardonius (as Herodotus alleges) or because events unfolded too quickly for him to bring his troops to bear. In either case, this left the

Persians with a *de facto* rear-guard which helped to cover the retreat of the rest of the army.

Secondly, the Persian cavalry was largely intact, having survived what was in the end an infantry v. infantry battle. The cavalry now acted as a screen, allowing the broken Persian infantry to stream through, but threatening sudden death to any Greek troops which advanced out of formation. As an example of what might happen if troops became disorganized, some soldiers from Megara were 'advancing in disorderly haste when they came to the notice of the Theban cavalry. The cavalry rode them down, killing 600 of them and chasing the rest to [the mountains of] Cithaeron.' (Herodotus *History* 9.69)

As ever, the casualty figures after the battle depend on who did the counting. Herodotus reckons that 250,000 Persians were killed for the loss of 159 Greeks. Since by his own report 600 Megarians alone also perished, it is clear that as his wont, Herodotus was only counting hoplites. Plutarch pours scorn on this figure, and points out that in the years after the battle the families of the Greek dead raised hundreds of personal memorials to the fallen, many of which were extant in his own time. Diodorus Siculus probably uses the now lost historian Ephorus to come to the figure of 10,000 Greek dead. This is not unrealistic if we assume that the Persian cavalry spent their time during the battle tearing through whatever Greek light infantry they caught out of position – for there were very many of these. Perhaps overall we can assume 9,000 dead among the Greek light infantry and 1,000 hoplites, of whom – says Herodotus – ninety-two were Spartan.

The casualty figures among the Persians vary even more widely because there were no families to claim the dead. Herodotus assumes that almost the entire Persian army perished, and for practical purposes he was correct. After Plataea, the army of Mardonius had ceased to exist, and with that army died the last possibility that Persia would threaten the Greek mainland.

To further emphasise this point, the Greeks later discovered that, purely by co-incidence, on the very day that the Persian army was being removed from existence at Plataea, the Persian navy was being excised from the Aegean Sea. The remnants of the Persian fleet had withdrawn from the coast of the Greek mainland. When their ships were eventually tracked down to the island of Samos by a vindictive allied fleet, the demoralized Persians did not even attempt battle at sea. Instead they beached their fleet and prepared to defend a stockade at the foot of Mount Mycale.

The Spartan king Leotychides led the Greek assault. As happened at more or less the same time at Plataea, the army had some trouble getting through the stockade. At this point their casualties were heavy, but once they were through the walls, the heavily-armoured hoplites wrought havoc among unarmoured Persians and more than evened the scales.

Epilogue

That day in high summer marked the end of Persian invasion. The victories of Plataea and Mycale also marked the apogee of Sparta as a Greek nation. At no time before or since was Sparta so powerful, so admired, feared and respected. 'All men know the right thing to do, but only the Spartans actually do it', ran a contemporary proverb. Throughout the Persian invasion the Greeks had looked to Sparta for leadership, and Sparta had delivered. The battle of Plataea demonstrated that even when that leadership was of poor quality, the superb training, discipline, courage and equipment of the average Spartan hoplite was enough to carry the day.

It was during the Persian wars that the legend of Sparta as a warrior nation grew to fruition. The Spartans themselves had assiduously cultivated that image for generations, but actually the nation's military record before the Persian Wars was unremarkable. The major military success of Sparta before the fifth century had been the conquest of Messenia, yet as has been argued in this book, at this time Sparta was a normal Greek city. The exceptional culture that Sparta developed was as a result of the need to hold on to Messenia, not the pressures involved in conquering the region in the first place.

Apart from Messenia, Sparta had mainly fought with its neighbour Argos, and with distinctly mixed fortunes. Certainly the Spartans got better as time went on, but for every major Spartan victory, the Argives could point to an earlier Spartan defeat. And Cleomenes, it will be remembered, had won his major victory over the Argives less through valour than through morally dubious subterfuge – the same sort of subterfuge that was the hallmark of Sparta's strategy through the Messenian wars.

Arguably what made Sparta great was not the nation's military prowess, but the fact that the early Spartans were relentless innovators. It would have horrified the conservative later Spartans to hear themselves described as such. Yet Sparta was among the first to adopt the system and armour of hoplite warfare. It was Sparta that first came up with the idea of a professional army, and Sparta that invented the unique *kleros* system to keep that army in the field. Sparta was centuries, if not millennia, ahead of other Greeks with its ideas for raising and educating girls. It was also the early Spartan talent for adaptation that allowed the Spartan kingship to remain as a political institution. Other nations jettisoned their kings in the Archaic Era. The Spartans were flexible and innovative enough to fit their kingship into a democracy which, though rudimentary, was still one of the most advanced in early Greece.

It was also the Spartans, when they discovered that it was near-impossible to expand their dominions beyond the headwaters of the Eurotas River, who hit upon the idea of hegemonic rule. Sixth-century Sparta dominated the rest of the Peloponnese through an innovative system of alliances that came to be known as the Peloponnesian League. The anti-Persian Hellenic League and the many different leagues in later Greece were loosely based on the Spartan model – but by that time Sparta had stopped innovating.

The Spartans drew the wrong lesson from their superb performance in resisting the Persian invasion. Rather than understanding that their state had become great through constant adaptation and the early adoption of new and radical ideas, the Spartans decided that their success was due to their 'unchanging' traditions and fixed laws.

This was all very well, but even just after Plataea, when Sparta basked in the admiration of the rest of Greece, the state faced acute social and demographic issues that needed fixing fast. Property was becoming concentrated in the hands of a small group of feuding elite families, the number of Spartiates was dropping alarmingly, and the Spartan economy was falling behind that of sophisticated mercantile states such as Corinth and Athens.

Early Sparta was capable of changing, and changing radically, to meet with new circumstances and challenges. Fifth-century Sparta was mesmerized by its own image of itself as a perfect, unchanging, brave and morally strong warrior state. This did Sparta no favours, because it meant that Sparta was not even prepared to recognize its fundamental problems, let alone fix them. Sparta was still to go on, and arguably to even greater strength in the coming decades. However, this strength was based on the momentum Sparta had been given by previous generations, and that momentum was already fading, as the later Spartans failed to build or change anything.

Classical Sparta remained perfectly suited to the conditions of the late sixth century, right up to the end of the second century BC. By that time it was a derided fossil, still geared up to fight the Persians of Xerxes in an age of international alliances and legionary warfare.

Select Bibliography

Aldrete, G.S., Bartell, S., Aldrete, A., *Reconstructing Ancient Linen Body Armor: Unraveling the Linothorax Mystery*, Johns Hopkins University Press, 2009.

Boardman, J., Hammond, L., Lewis, D.M., Ostwald, M. (eds.), *The Cambridge Ancient History Volume 4, Persia, Greece and the Western Mediterranean, c.525 to 479 BC*, Second Edition, Cambridge University Press, 1988.

Crawford, M., Whitehead, D., *Archaic and Classical Greece: A Selection of Ancient Sources in Translation*, Cambridge University Press, 1983.

Connolly, P., *Greece and Rome at War*, Macdonald, 1981.

Evans, J., 'Notes on Thermopylae and Artemisium', *Historia* 18, Stuttgart: Franz Steiner Verlag, Aug. 1969.

Figueira, T., *Spartan Society*, Classical Press of Wales, 2004.

Forrest, W.G., *A History of Sparta, 950–192 B.C.*, Norton & Company, 1969.

Hammond, N., 'Sparta at Thermopylae', *Historia* 45, Stuttgart: Franz Steiner Verlag, 1st Qtr., 1996.

Hendriks, I., 'The Battle of Sepeia', *Mnemosyne*, Fourth Series, Vol. 33, Fasc. 3/4, 1980.

Hunt, P., 'Helots at the Battle of Plataea' *Historia*, Stuttgart: Franz Steiner Verlag 2nd Qtr., 1997.

Huxley, G., *Early Sparta*, Irish Academic, Pr 1970.

Kelly, T., 'The Argive Destruction of Asine', *Historia*, Stuttgart: Franz Steiner Verlag, Sep. 1967.

Lazenby, J., *The Spartan Army*, Stackpole Books, 1985.

Morris, I., *Burial and Ancient Society: The Rise of the Greek City-*

State, New Studies in Archaeology: Cambridge University Press, 1990.

Pomeroy, S., *Spartan Women*, Oxford University Press, 2002.

Schwartz, A. 'Reinstating the Hoplite: Arms, Armour and Phalanx Fighting in Archaic and Classical Greece', *Historia* 207, Stuttgart: Franz Steiner Verlag, 2009.

Stibbe, C., *Das Andere Sparta*, Mainz, 1996.

Index

Index of Ancient Sources Discussed in the Text